Not Knowing Whither

The Steps of Abraham's Faith

*A Series of Studies
in the Life of Abraham*

by

Oswald Chambers

'Father, the narrow path
 To that far country show;
And in the steps of Abraham's faith
 Enable me to go.
A cheerful sojourner
 Where'er Thou bidst me roam,
Till, guided by Thy Spirit here,
 I reach my heavenly home.'

OSWALD CHAMBERS PUBLICATIONS
ASSOCIATION
and
MARSHALL, MORGAN & SCOTT
London : : Edinburgh

LONDON
MARSHALL, MORGAN AND SCOTT, LTD.,
33 LUDGATE HILL, E.C.4

AUSTRALIA
317 COLLINS STREET
MELBOURNE

NEW ZEALAND
23 MONTGOMERY ROAD
ROTHESAY BAY, AUCKLAND

SOUTH AFRICA
P.O. BOX 1720, STURK'S BUILDINGS
CAPE TOWN

CANADA
EVANGELICAL PUBLISHERS
366 BAY STREET
TORONTO

Reprinted 1957

Made and Printed in Great Britain by
Butler & Tanner Ltd., Frome and London

CONTENTS

PREFACE

THESE studies, from the lips of the late Oswald Chambers, are as wonderful as anything published by him hitherto. They concern the life of the great pioneer of the life of faith in which we see faith's reactions to God's call, to chastening circumstances, to the claims of companions, and to the terrific cost of God's friendship. Herein we see linked up, in a wonderful way, the experience of grace under the New Covenant with the eternal purpose of God made plain under the Old Covenant. Abraham is studied as a fore-runner of modern saints in their faith-walk.

The book is replete with spiritual wisdom. The very chapter titles betray that touch of genius, as men call it, which sparkles in the pages.

If great books are the life-blood of the world's master spirits, then such a book as this is the life-blood of one who by grace was brought to the fulness of the stature of Christ. The studies first appeared in the B.T.C. Journal. In book form they will make possible a term of guided reading on this outstanding example of the walk of faith in this world of men.

DAVID LAMBERT

PREFACE

THESE studies, from the lips of the late Oswald Chambers, are as wonderful as anything published by him hitherto. They concern the life of the great pioneer of the life of faith in which we see faith's reactions to God's call, to clashing circumstances, to the claims of companions, and to the terrific cost of God's Friendship. Herein we see linked up, in a wonderful way, the experience of grace under the New Covenant with the eternal purpose of God made plain under the Old Covenant. Abraham is studied as a forerunner of modern saints in their faith-walk.

The book is replete with spiritual wisdom. The very chapter titles betray that touch of genius, as men call it, which sparkles in the pages.

If great books are the life-blood of the world's master spirits, then such a book as this is the lifeblood of one who by grace was brought to the fulness of the stature of Christ. The studies first appeared in the *B.T.C. Journal*. In book form they will make possible a term of guided reading on this outstanding example of the walk of faith in this world of men.

DAVID LAMBERT

To

Our Mother

whose interest in the teaching field of
my husband's message has been an unfailing
source of inspiration — H.G.

To

Our Mother

*whose interest in the sending forth of
my husband's messages has been an unfailing
source of inspiration.—B.C.*

CROSSING THE BAR

Genesis xii. 1-3

"Sunset and evening star,
  And one clear call for me!
And may there be no moaning of the bar,
  When I put out to sea.

But such a tide as moving seems asleep,
  Too full for sound and foam,
When that which drew from out the boundless deep
  Turns again home.

Twilight and evening bell,
  And after that the dark!
And may there be no sadness of farewell,
  When I embark.

For tho' from out our bourne of Time and Place
  The flood may bear me far,
I hope to see my Pilot face to face
  When I have crost the bar."
                                    —Tennyson

'Now the Lord had said unto Abram, Get thee out.'

'Crossing the bar' is indicative of what happens whenever we act in faith in God. Whatever the faith is in connection with, we have to launch right out on God. To debate with God and trust common sense is moral blasphemy against God. The call of God embarrasses us because of two things—it presents us with sealed orders, and urges us to a vast venture. When God calls us He does not tell us along the line of our natural senses what to expect; God's call is a command that asks us, that means there is always a possibility of refusal on our part. Faith never knows where it is being led, it knows and loves the One Who is leading. It is a life of faith, not of intelligence and reason, but a life of knowing Who is making me go.

CROSSING THE BAR

Genesis xii. 1—3

'Sunset and evening star,
  And one clear call for me!
And may there be no moaning of the bar,
  When I put out to sea

But such a tide as moving seems asleep,
  Too full for sound and foam,
When that which drew from out the boundless deep
  Turns again home.

Twilight and evening bell,
  And after that the dark!
And may there be no sadness of farewell,
  When I embark;

For tho' from out our bourne of Time and Place
  The flood may bear me far,
I hope to see my Pilot face to face
  When I have crost the bar.'   *Tennyson*

'Now the Lord had said unto Abram, Get thee out. . . .'

'Crossing the bar' is indicative of what happens whenever we act in faith in God. Whatever the faith is in connection with, we have to launch right out on God. To debate with God and trust common sense is moral blasphemy against God. The call of God embarrasses us because of two things—it presents us with sealed orders, and urges us to a vast venture. When God calls us He does not tell us along the line of our natural senses what to expect; God's call is a command that *asks* us, that means there is always a possibility of refusal on our part. Faith never knows where it is being led, it knows and loves the One Who is leading. It is a life of *faith*, not of intelligence and reason, but a life of knowing Who is making me 'go'.

11

The personal private life of faith of each one of us has its source and explanation in the life of the Father of the Faithful, Abraham. Abraham's call, with his limitations as well as his obedience, is full of minute instruction with regard to the life of faith.

(1) THE CALL OF GOD

The call of God can never be stated explicitly, it is implicit. The call of God is like the call of the sea, or of the mountains; no one hears these calls but the one who has the nature of the sea or of the mountains; and no one hears the call of God who has not the nature of God in him. It cannot be definitely stated what the call of God is to, because it is a call into comradeship with God Himself for His own purposes, and the test of faith is to believe that God knows what He is after. The call of God only becomes clear as we obey, never as we weigh the *pros* and *cons* and try to reason it out. The call is God's idea, not our idea, and only on looking back over the path of obedience do we realize what is the idea of God; God sanctifies memory. When we hear the call of God it is not for us to dispute with God, and arrange to obey Him if He will expound the meaning of His call to us. As long as we insist on having the call expounded to us, we will never obey; but when we obey it is expounded, and in looking back there comes a chuckle of confidence—'He doeth all things well.' Before us there is nothing, but overhead there is God, and we have to trust Him. If we insist on explanations before we obey, we lie like clogs on God's plan and put ourselves clean athwart His purpose.

> 'To do our best is one part, but to wash our hands smilingly of the consequences is the next part of any sensible virtue.'
>
> *Robert Louis Stevenson*

When Jesus Christ says 'Follow Me', He never says to where, the consequences must be left entirely to

Him. We come in with our 'buts', and 'supposings', and 'what will happen if I do?' (cf. Luke ix. 57—62.) We have nothing to do with what will happen if we obey, we have to abandon to God's call in unconditional surrender and smilingly wash our hands of the consequences. Until we get through all the shivering wisdom that will not venture out on God, we will never know all that is involved in the life of faith. Fate means stoical resignation to an unknown force. Faith is not resignation to a power we do not know; faith is committal to One Whose character we do know because it has been revealed to us in Jesus Christ. As we live in contact with God, His order comes to us in the haphazard, and we recognize that every detail of our lives is engineered for us by our Heavenly Father. If we are going to live a life of faith, we must rest nowhere until we see God and know Him in spite of all apparent contradictions.

> 'I have to take care not to settle on the sandbank of selfishness, but to leave all for the Lord to order it. If I then make shipwreck, it will be in the wide sea of God's love, the depths of which are as welcome to me as the surest haven. But nature fights against the thought of venturing forth we know not where, out of self, into unknown regions.'   *Tersteegen*

(II) THE CALLING OF ABRAHAM

'Now the Lord had said unto Abram, Get thee out . . .' '. . . and he went out, not knowing whither he went.' This is true of a fool or of a faithful soul. One of the hardest lessons to learn is the one brought out by Abraham's obedience to the call of God. He went 'out' of all his own ways of looking at things and became a fool in the eyes of the world. In the beginning faith is always uncertain, because every broad view is at first an uncertain view of

13

particulars. We hear the call of God while we listen to a sermon, or during a time of prayer, and we say— 'Yes, I will give myself to God unreservedly.' Then something happens in our immediate circumstances which does not seem to fit into the vision we have had, and the danger is that we compromise and say we must have been mistaken in the vision. We have to stand true to the fact of God's call and smilingly wash our hands of the consequences. We have nothing to do with the afterwards of obedience. It is easy to want to be always on the mount, but when we come down to the devil-possessed valley we get annoyed or exhausted, we cannot go on with God there. We have perfect faith in God as long as He keeps us on the mount, but not the slightest atom of faith when He takes us into the valley. We have to be careful that the things which are really impertinent actualities do not find us either ignoring them or abandoning our faith in God. We have to go through the trial of our faith in these particulars, because it is the trial of our faith that makes us wealthy towards God.

'And from thy kindred . . .' Personal acquaintance with God shows itself in separation, symbolized by Abraham's physical separation from his country and his kindred. Nowadays it means much more a moral separation from the way those nearest and dearest to us think and look at things, if, that is, they have not a personal relationship with God. Jesus emphasized this (see Luke xiv. 26). Arguers against obeying the call of God will arise in the shape of country and kindred, and if you listen to them you will soon dull your ears to God's call and become the dullest, most commonplace Christian imaginable, because you have no courage in your faith; you have seen and heard, but have not gone on. If you accept sympathy from those who have not heard the call of God, it will so blunt your own sense of His call that you become useless to Him. Every saint must stand out absolutely

14

alone. Beware lest the sympathy of others competes with God for the throne of your life. Don't look for a comrade other than God when God speaks to you; through *you* will come His purpose.

Genesis xii. 4—9.

'Not of the sunlight,
Not of the moonlight,
Not of the starlight!
O young Mariner,
Down to the haven,
Call your companions,
Launch your vessel,
And crowd your canvas,
And, ere it vanishes
Over the margin,
After it, follow it,
Follow The Gleam.'

Tennyson

'So Abram departed.'

It is not sin or disobedience only that keeps us from obeying the call of God, but the good, right, natural things that make us hesitate. The natural can only be transformed into the spiritual by obedience, and the beginnings of God's life in a man or woman cut directly across the will of nature. The sword has to go through the natural (*Cf.* Luke ii. 35). The call of God comes with a realization that what God says is true, but that does not prevent us from going through the trial of our faith in connection with actual details, and it is when we touch actual details that we begin to dispute with God and say—'But if I obeyed God here, my sense of justice and right would be injured.' To talk in that way means we do not believe God one atom, although we say we do. The knowledge of God's will is not in the nature of a mathematical problem; as we obey, we make out what is His will, it becomes as clear as daylight. We have to be continually renewed in the spirit of our minds, refusing to be conformed to the spirit of the age in which we live, then we shall 'prove'—literally, make out in obedience—'what is that good, and acceptable, and perfect will of God.' We have to beware of giving credit to man's wisdom for the way he has taken, when all the time it is the perfect wisdom of God that is manifested through the simple obedience of the man. It is never the acute ability of the saint that is exhibited, but the astute wisdom of God.

(I) THE CONCESSION OF ABRAHAM'S FAITH. v. 4

We must remember that faith in God always demands a concession from us personally. 'So Abram departed,' that is, he went on with God as God had commanded him, 'not knowing whither he went.' Watch the debates that go on in our minds when God speaks, whether it is in a big or a little matter, we won't launch out on God's word, we will hug the shore line. 'But it is so unwise to trust God in this matter'—that implies that God has no wisdom at all. If we are going to obey God there must be a concession made on our part; we have deliberately to trust the character of God as it has been revealed to us in the face of all obstacles. 'If God would only come down and explain everything to me, I would have faith in Him,' we say; and yet how little trust we are inclined to have in God, even when we have had an experience of His grace and a revelation of Himself. We sink back to the experience instead of being confident in the God Who gave us the experience. Experience is never the ground of our trust, it is the gateway to the One Whom we trust. The work of faith is not an explanation to our minds, but a determination on our part to obey God and to make a concession of our faith in His character; immediately we do what God says, we discern what He means. Naturally, man is made to have dominion, therefore he insists on explanations, because everything we can explain we can command. In the spiritual domain nothing is explained until we

17

obey, and then it is not so much an explanation as an instant discernment. 'If any man *will do* . . . he shall *know* . . .' If we say 'I want to know why I should do this,' it means we have no faith in God, but only sordid confidence in our own wits. 'If God would only give me supernatural touches, I would trust Him.' No, we would idolize ourselves. 'I do not mind being a saint if I can remain natural and be a saint entirely on my own initiative. If I can instruct God about my upbringing and my particular temperament and affinities, and construct my own scenery, then I would like to be a saint.' All along it is the hesitation of the natural refusing to be transformed into the spiritual. In Abraham there was no hesitation, although there were misinterpretations. In the life of Our Lord there was no hesitation and no misinterpretations; He combined the great vision of faith with the actual details. The Apostle Paul always applies the great eternal truths to actual details, because that is where faith has to work. The characteristic of Abraham's faith was that he did not select his affinities, he made a concession of his faith to God, and 'went out, not knowing whither he went.'

(II) THE COMPANIONS OF ABRAHAM'S FAITH. v. 5

If God has given you a personal revelation of Himself and you have made a distinct concession on your part of faith in His character, you will make a great blunder if you look to see whether others see the same thing. God will undertake to instruct them if you remain faithful to the immediate connections in which He has put you. To live a life alone with God does not mean that we live it apart from everyone else. The connection between godly men and women and those associated with them is continually revealed in the Bible, e.g., 1 Timothy iv. 10. If you are going on with God, says Paul, your attitude is to 'labour and suffer reproach' from those who because of apparently accidental relationships go with you, so that by your labour you may bring them to be among the conscious believers. There is a difference between conscious and unconscious salvation. To be consciously saved means that we become of immense practical value to God in this order of things.

(III) THE CONSECRATION OF ABRAHAM'S FAITH. v. 6-9

Notice the significance of v. 8—'there he builded an altar unto the Lord.' Worship is the tryst of sacramental identification with God, that is, I deliberately give back to God the best He has given me that I may be identified with Him in it. Whenever Abraham neglected to build an altar after God had made a promise to him, he fell into sin. Every act of worship to be effective must be a public testimony to those who in God's providence are with us for worship; it is at once the most public and the most personally sacred act that God demands of His faithful ones. Whenever God has given you a blessing, take time to meditate beside the blessing and offer it back to God in a deliberate ecstasy of worship. God will never allow you to hold a spiritual blessing for yourself, it has to be given back to Him that He may make it a blessing to others. If you hoard it, it will turn to spiritual dry rot. If God has blessed you, erect an altar and give the blessing back to God as a love-gift.

Abraham 'pitched his tent, having Beth-el on the west and Hai on the east.' Beth-el is the symbol of communion with God; Hai is the symbol of the world: Abraham pitched his tent between the two. The measure of the worth of our public activity to God is the private, profound communion we have with Him. Rush is always wrong; there is plenty of time to worship God. There are not three stages—worship, waiting and work; some of us go in jumps like spiritual frogs, we jump from worship to waiting and from waiting to work. God's idea is that the three should go together; they were always together in the life of Our Lord, He was unhasting and unresting. It is a discipline, we cannot get there all at once.

THE DANCE OF CIRCUMSTANCES

Gen. xii. 10—13

'Not for such hopes and fears
Annulling youth's brief years,
Do I remonstrate: folly wide the mark!
Rather I prize the doubt
Low kinds exist without,
Finished and finite clods, untroubled by a spark.

: : : . :

Then, welcome each rebuff
That turns earth's smoothness rough,
Each sting that bids nor sit nor stand but go!
Be our joy three-parts pain!
Strive, and hold cheap the strain;
Learn, nor account the pang; dare, never grudge the
throe!'

Browning

'And there was a famine in the land.' v. 10

There is a difference between circumstances and
environment. We cannot control our circumstances,
but we are the deciders of our own environment.
Environment is the element in our circumstances
which fits the disposition. A man convicted of sin
and a man in love may be in the same external
circumstances, but the environment of the one is
totally different from that of the other. Our environment depends upon our personal reaction to circumstances. 'Circumstances over which I have no control'
is a perfectly true phrase, but it must never be made
to mean that we cannot control ourselves in those
circumstances. No matter into what perplexing
circumstances God's providence may lead us or allow
us to go, we have to see to it that in our reaction to
those circumstances, which dance around us so
perplexingly, we exhibit a personal relation to the

21

highest we know. It is only by living in the presence of God that we cease to act in an ungodlike manner in perplexing circumstances.

(I) THE FAMINE IN THE LAND OF PROMISE. v. 10

This must have been a severe test to Abraham's faith. Take it personally: we hear God's word on the mount, but when it comes to the dance of circumstances we are 'knocked out', because we forget that we have to react in those circumstances in accordance with our faith in God. In going down to Egypt, Abraham declined from this standard.

The element of discipline in the life of faith must never be lost sight of, because only by means of the discipline are we taught the difference between the natural interpretation of what we call good and what God means by 'good'. We have to be brought to the place of hearty agreement with God as to what He means by good, and we only reach it by the trial of our faith, never by a stoical effort, such as saying—'Well, I must make up my mind that this is God's will, and that it is best.'

At times it appears as if God has not only forsaken His word, but has deliberately deceived us. We asked Him for a particular thing, or related ourselves to Him along a certain line, and expected that it would mean the fulness of blessing, and actually it has meant the opposite—upset, trouble and difficulty all around, and we are staggered, until we learn that by this very discipline God is bringing us to the place of entire abandonment to Himself.

Never settle down in the middle of the dance of circumstances and say that you have been mistaken in your natural interpretation of God's promise to you because the immediate aftermath is devastation; say that God did give you the promise, and stick to it, and slowly God will bring you into the perfect, detailed fulfilment of that promise. When and where the fulfilment will take place, depends upon God and yourself, but never doubt the absolute fulfilment of God's word, and remember that the beginning of the fulfilment lies in your acquiescence in God's will. Remain true to God, although it means the sword going through the natural, and you will be brought into a supernaturally clear agreement with God. We are not introduced to Christianity by explanations, but we must labour at the exposition of Christianity until we satisfactorily unfold it through God's grace and our own effort.

(II) THE FOREBODING ON THE LINE OF PEACE. v. 11-13

In the beginning of the life of faith the first element is that of fanaticism. There must be the cutting off, and the maiming, and the separation. There is nothing fascinating about any of that, but when the life has become imbedded in God, and the maiming has disappeared into the full-orbed perfection of a child of God, then that perfection has a tremendous fascination for others even though they do not care anything about God. Then comes the danger of this subterfuge—'I won't tell other people the whole truth, I won't say I am delivered from all sin, or sanctified wholly, that is too rugged, it will offend them; I will cover up the vital testimony and say I am religiously inclined, then I shall be able to preserve my influence with them.' Whenever that cunning rascal 'expediency' comes in, it will bring in its train a foreboding anxiety, which is a sure sign that in that particular we are ceasing to obey God. Our testimony must be unmistakably to the whole of the truth, not to part of it only. It is impossible to go on in our life with God if the element of personal testimony is left out; we will begin to get dexterous with a dexterity that is more or less doubtful, we say the truth but not the

23

whole truth. Whenever God reveals something which we have never seen before and which affects others, a public testimony must be made, and the peril is lest we say—'But if I stand up and give that testimony, other people will be stumbled.' Whenever we start this doubtful weighing of things we are acting not in accordance with our reliance on God, but in presumptuous confidence that God will see us through if we trust our wits: God will see us through only if we stand stedfastly true to what He has told us. Another danger is to imagine that it is my particular presentation of things that will attract people. It may attract them, but never to God. The line of attraction is always an indication of the goal of the attracted; if you attract by personal impressiveness, the attracted will get no further than you. Our Lord said—'*I*, if *I* be lifted up, will draw all men unto Me.'

v. 13 reveals a weakness in Abraham's faith, he does not yet perfectly rely upon the help of God in God's own way and time. This weakness arises from the inability to apply our faith in God to the actual circumstances we are in. We have to be true to God, not true only to our idea of God.

> 'The failures of the chosen men of God upon a closer examination reveal them as sins of weakness arising from unguarded strength, which failures on the one hand do not destroy the personal standing with God, but on the other hand render necessary in him a purifying and providential training.'
>
> *Foster's Essay on 'The Aversion of Men*
> *of Taste to Evangelical Religion.'*

If we imagine we have strength apart from God, we shall have to break the neck of our strength over some obstacle before we are willing to rely upon God. Our own strength is the backbone of the natural life, but if the backbone of the strength of the natural man is removed without planting in the backbone of the life of God, there will be the 'wobble', which persists until the vision of faith and the reality are one and the same.

BLANK ASTONISHMENT

Ch. xii. 14—20

'Pure faith indeed—you know not what you ask!
Naked belief in God the Omnipotent,
Omniscient, Omnipresent, sears too much
The sense of conscious creatures to be borne.
It were the seeing him, no flesh shall dare.
. . . . . .
No, when the fight begins within himself,
A man's worth something. God stoops o'er his head,
Satan looks up between his feet—both tug—
He's left, himself, i' the middle: the soul wakes
And grows. Prolong that battle through his life!
Never leave growing till the life to come!'

Browning

'What is this that thou hast done unto me?' v. 18

When we sin directly, we are never blankly astonished at the result. We may be defiant, we may tell lies; or, what is better, we may accept God's forgiveness. Blank astonishment always comes because of failure to do God's will by our very desire to do it. There is no word of censure on Abraham in the Bible for his distinct failure in going down to Egypt on account of the famine in the land God had promised him; but the blank astonishment which it caused is implied all through. Beware of saying what Abraham ought to have done—firstly, because he did not do it; and secondly, because you increase the severity of your own condemnation. This incident is not related for the dishonour of Abraham, but for the honour of God. Abraham did not attempt to vindicate himself.

Beware of thinking (no matter what you say) that God guided you in your decisions; the thought leads to spiritual hypocrisy. God holds His children responsible for the way in which they interpret His will. We only discern God's will by being renewed in the spirit of our minds in every circumstance we are in. We must learn to tell ourselves the truth on the basis of God's word, not on the basis of independent spiritual impulse, although by our blunders of impulse we are chastened as God's sons and daughters.

(1) THE SAINT'S GUILT IN THE WORLDLING'S SIN.
v. 14—16

The result of Abraham's going down to Egypt was perplexity to himself, and he was also responsible for bringing a direct occasion of sin to Pharaoh. Pharaoh treats Abraham with a generosity which must have put Abraham to shame.

Get alarmed when your desire to serve God brings you into such a position that you have to accept, because you cannot refuse, the magnanimous treatment of worldlings who do not know your Lord; because to be in that position means you have transgressed God's order by the very keenness of your desire to do His will; and when you withdraw, as you must do ultimately, it will be with the knowledge that you have been the direct occasion of sin to them.

Christian work is apt to lead individual saints into blank astonishment, because it springs from an eager desire to do God's will. To say—'I want to do God's will,' is to put myself outside God altogether. The striking thing in Our Lord's life was that He was not more eager to do the will of His Father than His Father was for Him to do it. He was the Saviour of the world, everything depended upon Him, and yet for thirty years He did nothing wonderful. 'His doing nothing wonderful was in itself a kind of wonder' (*Bonaventura*). Our Lord's life is the exhibition of *the will of God*, not of *doing* the will of God.

Beware in your judgment either on Abraham or on yourself that you do not transfer the judgment to a stage of moral development not yet reached. It is easy to exaggerate. For example, an act that would

27

be criminal in a man is not criminal in a boy. Abraham's transgression must never be classed as a sin morally. He transgressed through eagerness to do the right thing. Transgression is nearly always an unconscious act, there is no conscious determination to do wrong; sin is never an unconscious act. We blunder when we refuse to discern between these two.

(II) THE SAINT'S GIFTS FROM THE WORLDLING'S SINCERITY. v. 16

The Egyptian maid Hagar, who became so important an influence in the lives of Abraham and Sarah, was probably amongst the gifts which came to Abraham in Egypt. The friendships and gifts of the world are perfectly sincere, but the saint soon realizes that these friendships and gifts are embarrassing and hindering if he is to remain loyal to God. Then begins the blank astonishment of real perplexity, and God never shields us from anxiety on this score. It is not a case of right and wrong, but of learning through chastening what Abraham learned, that we cannot come eagerly and find out God's will by guessing. We must be renewed in our minds in every circumstance we are in, and beware of suspicions and considerations and suggestions that make themselves seem right to us. Beware of despising the chastening of the Lord, or of fainting when you are rebuked of Him. The only thing to do is to take your blank astonishment, be silent about it, and go on to the next thing.

(III) THE SAINT'S GROANING AND THE WORLDLING'S SCORN. v. 17—18

Pharaoh is a better man than those around him, and he concludes directly that the judgment on his house is from God on account of Sarah, whose person God is guarding as the true mother of Israel. Abraham did not tell a lie, he told a half-truth (see Gen. xx. 12)

28

To say that if a man is committing sin he will hinder the purpose of God, is not true; if a *leader* is trying to serve his own ends, he will hinder the purpose of God. For instance, if I were to try and utilize this house of God for my own ends, the atmosphere of the house would be damaged instantly. Personal sin does not present a barrier in God's house, although it does put a barrier between the one who is sinning and God; but immediately anyone tries to utilize God's house, or God's people, or God's things for his own purposes and ends, then the atmosphere is altered at once. Then the thoughts of many hearts are revealed and there is produced the groaning of the saints and the scorn of the worldling, and the humiliating thing is that in such a case the worldling is right.

(IV) THE SAINT'S GRADE IN THE WORLDLING'S SEPARATION. v. 19—20

Abraham was dismissed by Pharaoh—a most unspeakable humiliation. If you have made a compromise out of your eagerness to stand for God's honour, you will have to endure to the last limit, as Abraham did, the scorn of the honourable worldling. Instead of your breaking from the world, the world will come with all its courtesy and say—Will you go? By your very desire to stand up loyally for God, you have put yourself in a position where you cannot stand up for Him. The discipline of our lives is to become as little children. A little child would have stayed in the land whether there was a famine or not.

Abraham's going down to Egypt, and his 'dumbfoundering' there, is the reason for all the complexity that came afterwards, and accounts for the continual recurrence of Egypt in the history of the Kingdom of God, until at last Egypt is to be united into the great, full purpose of God.

UNPERPLEXED

Ch. xiii

'Yea, this in him was the peculiar grace
    (Hearten our chorus!)
That before living he'd learn how to live—
    No end to learning:
Earn the means first—God surely will contrive
    Use for our earning.
Others mistrust and say, "But time escapes:
    Live now or never!"
He said, "What's time? Leave Now for dogs and apes!
    Man has Forever".'   *Browning*

'. . . unto the place of the altar, which he had made
there at the first.' v. 4

When we come to study the lives of the saints, the
confusing thing is that from one standpoint they are a
jumble of inconsistencies, whilst from another standpoint they are an exhibition of the boundless consistency of God. This needs to be heeded, because if
we study the life of a saint in order to find out what
God is like, we shall finish up in the dumps and
say—It is enough; whereas if we study God Himself,
we shall find that He manifests His amazing consistency in the weakest and feeblest saint. At one time
we find Abraham in a blank and sordid muddle; at
another, we find him unperplexed and noble. The
point is that God remains the same whether Abraham
is unperplexed or muddled.

(1) THE TRYST OF SACRAMENTAL IDENTIFICATION. v.
    1—4
    Abraham went with God, and Lot 'went with
Abraham.' Lot went down to Egypt with Abraham,
and came back with Abraham, and the abundance
of their possessions nearly brought about strife. A life

of *faithfulness* is devotion to a servant or handmaid of God; a life of *faith* is devotion to God. Lot continually went to pieces; Abraham never did.

The Way. We have to keep tryst with God in contact with the peculiar ways of everyone, and this can only be done by sacramental identification. The one thing Our Lord heeded was His tryst with God in connection with everyone, whether it was Judas or Peter or John; He took no account of the evil. We get huffed in no time—'No, they did not treat me rightly;' 'they did not consider that I ought to have been considered.' Will I keep my tryst with God in contact with the blackguard or the traitor or the saint? Whoever it is, is nothing to do with me. I have not to fit other people into my ideas, but to keep tryst with God in relation to them. I am not to ignore them, but to refuse to look at them from my idea of what they ought to be, and to look at them only as facts in relation to my tryst with God.

The Wealth. Abraham came back exceedingly wealthy, but he kept tryst with God over his possessions. Beware of not keeping tryst with God over your possessions, whether they be material or not. It is perilously possible not to, but to make your spiritual life depend on the abundance of things you possess. If God has given you the wealth of Divine healing for your body, keep tryst with Him over it. When you are learning to trust God, He gives you at first certain things you lean on; then He withdraws, and you say it is the devil. No, it is the chastening of the Lord because He sees that you are possessing those things. You can only possess your possessions by being detached from them to God Who is the Source. If you are drawing your life from God and begin to take a wrong line, God will withdraw His life. This is also true with regard to money. We have only one Source, and that is God. One of the biggest snares is the idea that God is sure to lead us to success.

31

The Worship. All commentators notice one interesting point in Abraham's life, viz. the times he erected an altar and the times he did not; whenever he neglected to erect an altar, he went astray. This fact is one of great significance because worship is the tryst of sacramental identification. In worship I deliberately give back to God the best He has given me that I may be identified with Him in it. If Abraham had erected an altar, he would not have gone down to Egypt, but would have identified himself with God over the famine in the land of promise. Selfishness in spiritual matters produces delusion rapidly. If in every case of blank astonishment, we go back to the place where we first built an altar to God, we will be delivered from the delusion of obtuse independent certainty. Worship is the sacramental element in the saint's life.

(II) THE TEST OF SELF INTEREST. v. 5—13

As surely as we begin our life of faith with God, fascinating, luxurious and rich prospects will open to us, which are ours by right, but if we are living the life of faith we will exercise the right to waive our rights and give them away, letting God choose for us. It is the discipline of transforming the natural into the spiritual by obedience to God's voice. In the life of faith God allows us to get into a place of testing where the consideration of our own welfare would be the right and proper thing if we were not living the life of faith; but if we are living the life of faith, we will heartily waive our own rights in favour of those whose right it is not, and leave God to choose for us. Whenever we make 'right' our guidance, we blunt our spiritual insight. The greatest enemy of the life with God is not sin, but the good that is not good enough. It would seem the wisest thing in the world for Abraham to choose, it was his right, and the people round him would consider him a fool for not choosing. Many of us do not go on in our spiritual life because we prefer to choose what is our right instead of relying upon God to choose for us. We have to learn to walk according to the standard that has its eye on God.

The Tax of Riches. v. 5—7. Abraham's riches were in a great measure a tax to him. Every possession is tainted with a want; in this case the want was for sufficient pasturage. When Jesus Christ came He possessed nothing; the only symbol for our Lord is the symbol of poverty (2 Cor. viii. 9; Luke ix. 58) and this is true of the saint—'having nothing, and yet possessing all things.' Every possession produces an appetite that clings.

The Touch of Rectitude. Lot forgot the place of communion, he thought only of the world. But Abraham, unperplexed, instantly exhibited forbearance as the result of his tryst with God, he walked in the moral atmosphere of the Sermon on the Mount. Abraham's rectitude was not the rectitude of honour, but of holiness. This rectitude is exhibited in the life of Jesus Christ, of Whom it is recorded that He 'pleased not Himself.' This gives the deathblow to subjectivity, that is, to the subjective experiences based on what is pleasing to my holy self; of the holiest Being Who ever trod this earth it is recorded that He pleased not Himself.

The Tarnish of Reasonableness. v. 10—13. Lot chose what he considered the best for his possessions. This is the tarnish of reasonableness of a mind that has neglected its tryst with God.

(III) THE TYPE OF SUPREME INTEGRITY. v. 14—18

We must distinguish between the times when God revealed Himself to Abraham and the times when He concealed Himself. In the former, Abraham's faith is elevated; in the latter it sinks.

The Manifestation of God. v. 14. The first manifestation of God to Abraham was in his migration to Canaan;

the first concealing when he went down to Egypt. Abraham did not have another manifestation of God until after his noble act of faith toward Lot.

The Message of God. v. 15—16. The promises of God correspond to the acts and conduct of faith in Abraham. Only when Abraham acts in accordance with his real faith in God, does God speak to him. There is a connection throughout between the providence of God and the conduct of Abraham.

The Man of God. v. 18. Paul takes Abraham as a type of the life of faith, not as the type of a saint, but of a tried faith built on a real God. The sanctification of our faith, as distinct from the sanctification of our heart, is the unfathomable, supernatural blessing from God.

WAR

Gen. xiv. 1—16

'Let it go or stay, so I wake to the higher aims
Of a land that has lost for a while her lust of gold,
And love of a peace that was full of wrongs and
    shames,
Horrible, hateful, monstrous, not to be told;
And hail once more to the banner of battle unroll'd!
Tho' many a light shall darken, and many shall
    weep
For those that are crush'd in the clash of jarring
    claims. . . .
Let it flame or fade, and the war roll down like a
    wind,
We have proved we have hearts in a cause, we are
    noble still,
And myself have awaked, as it seems, to the better
    mind;
It is better to fight for the good than to rail at the
    ill;
I have felt with my native land, I am one with my
    kind,
I embrace the purpose of God, and the doom
    assign'd.'   *Tennyson*

'. . . and he told Abram the Hebrew; . . . he armed
his trained servants.' v. 13—14.

In the study of Abraham, as in the study of all
Bible characters, principles are no guide. The inconsistencies which we find in Abraham reveal the
consistency of God, and the thing to note is that
Abraham remained true to God both before and
after his lapses. Beware, however, what you call
lapses in Abraham. For instance, there is no lapse on
Abraham's part in connection with this war, but
rather the presentation of the inspiration of God. Error
lies in making the basis of truth an abstraction, or a

35

principle, instead of a personal relationship. Reality is not found in logic; Reality is a Person. '*I am the Truth.*' Spiritual life is based on a personal relationship to Jesus Christ, and on the consequent responsibility of that relationship.

(I) THE WAR OF VIOLENCE. v. 1—8

This is the first war mentioned in Scripture, and its cause was the lust for dominion. The war of the world against the world is portrayed in this chapter, and it is full of the most intense spiritual interpretation. Life without conflict is impossible, either in nature or in grace. This is an open fact of life. The basis of physical, mental, moral and spiritual life is antagonism. Physical life is maintained according to the power of fight in the corpuscles of the blood. If I have sufficient vital force within to overcome the forces without, I produce the balance of health. The same is true of mental life. If I want to maintain a clear, vigorous, mental life, I have to fight, and in this way I produce the balance of thought. Morally it is the same. Virtue is the result of fight; I am only virtuous according to the moral stability I have within. If I have sufficient moral fighting capacity, I produce the moral balance of virtue. We make virtue out of necessity, but no one is virtuous who is good because he cannot help it. Virtue is the outcome of conflict. And spiritually it is the same. 'In the world ye shall have tribulation'; i.e., everything that is not spiritual makes for my undoing; 'but be of good cheer; I have overcome the world.' When once this is understood it is a perfect delight to meet opposition, and as we learn to score off the things that come against us, we produce the balance of holiness. Faith must be tried, and it is the trial of faith that is precious. If you are faint-hearted, it is a sign you won't play the game, you are fit for neither God nor man because you will face nothing.

When God's providence involves us unexpectedly in all sorts of complications, the test comes on two lines—Will I have faith in God; and will I ally myself with those who rescue the down-trodden irrespective of their beliefs? It is instructive to note in the Bible that faint-heartedness arises whenever self-interest begins to get luxurious. The sign of faint-heartedness in individuals is in the languid talk of 'someone else' when there is anything to be done.

Whenever there is the experience of fag or weariness or degradation, you may be certain you have done one of two things—either you have disregarded a law of nature, or you have deliberately got out of touch with God. There is no such thing as weariness in God's work. If you are in tune with the joy of God, the more you spend out in God's service, the more the recuperation goes on, and when once the warning note of weariness is given, it is a sign that something has gone wrong. If only we would heed the warning, we would find it is God's wonderfully gentle way of saying—'Not that way; that must be left alone; this must be given up.' Spiritual fatigue comes from the unconscious frittering away of God's time. When you feel weary or are exhausted, don't ask for hot milk, but get back to God. The secret of weariness and nervous disease in the natural world is the lack of a dominating interest, and the same is true in spiritual life. Much of what is called Christian work is veneered spiritual disease; it is Christian activity that counts—dominating life from God, and every moment is filled with an energy that is not our own, a super-abounding life that nothing can stand before.

(III) THE WAR OF DIVINE INSPIRATION. v. 13—16

In Ch. xiii Abraham was put through the test of self-interest, and here he is put through the test of self-complacency. The occasion for self-complacency

would be in seeing that what befell Lot was just, and
that God was proving Abraham to be in the right. But
Abraham did not go under in the test; he did not sit
down, as it were, with a sanctified smirk and say,
'Perhaps he will learn wisdom now.' Abraham entered
into the war with the light and cheerful heroism of
heaven.

'. . . servants, born in his own house.' This phrase
is of great spiritual significance. Whenever a conflict
takes place, such as is pictured here, the successful
fighters are the faithful children of the faithful saints.
In spiritual warfare may God have mercy on the
barren saint who has never produced his own kind
but has to rely upon the converts of others. In the
rugged details of the Old Testament regarding marriage, there is always a spiritual revelation. In the
natural world there are three—father, mother and
child; and in the spiritual world there are three—
God, Church and converts. If a spiritual nature
cannot reproduce its own kind, it will have to answer
to God for it. If you have to rely in times of stress
upon the converts of others, the conflict drags out
desperately; you can always rely on your own
converts, those whom you have been the means of
leading into the truth.

MORE THAN CONQUEROR

Genesis xiv. 17—24

'Why have we yet no great deliverance wrought,
  Why have we not truth's banner yet unfurled,
High floating in the face of all the world,—
Why do we live and yet accomplish nought?
  What time the years pass from us of our youth,
  And we unto the altar of high truth
As yet no worthy offering have brought.
But now we bid these restless longings cease;
  If Heaven has aught for us to do or say,
Our time will come; and we may well hold peace,
  When He, till thrice ten years had passed away,
In stillness and in quietness upgrew,
Whose word once spoken should make all things new.'

Trench

'Now consider how great this man was, unto whom even the patriarch Abraham gave the tenth of the spoils.' Hebrews vii. 4.

We have to live perfectly actual lives, not actually perfect lives. This fact makes all the difference between religious faith and religious farce, and is very clearly brought out in the life of Abraham. God is not actual, He is real, and He bears into me His Holy Spirit Who enables me to live a perfectly actual life, kept by the reality of the love of God. 'I don't feel this and that'—how can you when God is not actual, but real? Feeling has to do with actualities and will come later. Right feeling is produced by obedience, never vice versa. I am brought into contact with actuality by my senses, and into contact with reality by my faith. The test in actual things is—Am I living a life of faith, or a life of common sense which denies faith? Faith does not make me *actually perfect*; faith makes me *perfectly actual*.

39

(I) WHEN THE VICTORY IS WON. v. 17

The supreme test in the perfectly actual life of faith comes after a victory has been gained, because in the expansive hour of relaxation the ruling disposition of the heart is instantly manifested. We read of Our Lord that after a day when 'all the city was gathered together at the door,' He rose up a great while before day in order to pray, not to praise (Mark i. 32—35). In Abraham the victory revealed that he was more than conqueror over himself. To say 'I have got the victory' is a selfish testimony; the testimony of the Spirit of God is that the Victor has got me. If we can notify victories for ourselves, we are not in right relationship to God at that particular time. Instead of worshipping God we are conscious only of what He has done through us, and we triumph in the experience He has brought us. My actual life is given me by God, and I can live in it either as an atheist or as a worshipper. Abraham stands as one who worships God after a victory.

(II) WHERE THE VICTOR IS A WORSHIPPER. v. 18—20

Just where Abram stands as the most striking character, Melchizedek enters and towers above him.

'What better type or symbol could there be of the absolute, the everlasting, because the divine, high priesthood and kingship than that phenomenal figure of Melchizedek? He comes out of the invisible, timeless eternity of the past; he belongs to the timeless assured eternity of the future; he is High Priest forever.' *Du Bose*

Melchizedek is a type of Christ; Abraham is never taken as a type of Christ, he is a type of the perfectly actual children of God. Melchizedek represents the Incarnation of God; Abraham represents the life of faith in the God Who became Incarnate. 'Christ in me' and 'I in Christ'; 'Christ the Lord' and 'Christ the

40

Servant'—all become simple when we understand the relationship of Melchizedek and Abraham.

The supreme lesson of the perfectly actual life of faith is to learn how to worship. Faith brings me into personal contact with God before Whom I must ever bow. I have to maintain a worshipful relationship to God in everything, and in the beginning this is difficult. I am all right at meetings, at anything that is illuminated, but when it comes to actual life, I am actually of no use. I can talk till further orders, but don't ask me to live the life.

We have to contend for God in our actual circumstances, and our contention for God lies in seeing that we rely upon Him absolutely while we carry out the dictates of our faith in Him. Melchizedek brings bread and wine to refresh the heroes of the perfectly actual life. Christ never takes part in the perfectly actual mix-up of our human lives; therefore to ask 'What would Jesus do?' is not the question of faith, but of Pharisaism. The question to ask is—*'What would Jesus have me do?'* It is impossible for Christ to be where you are, that is why He has put you there. You have to put on the new man in the actual circumstances you are in and manifest Him. It is arrogant humbug to imagine we are to be God Almighty on this earth. We are to be the sons and daughters of God, to live actual lives and put on the new man by deliberate acts of faith all the time, not denying the actual life. We have to remember that our bodies are the temples of the Holy Ghost, and to see that God is manifested in our mortal flesh by our worship; and that can only be done as we take the nourishment, the bread and the wine, which will sustain us in our actual contentions for God. 'For in that He Himself hath suffered being tempted, He is able to succour them that are tempted,' i.e., succour us with His bread and wine in the hour of our temptation (Heb. ii. 18 and iv. 15).

It is dangerous to take Abraham as the picture of

sanctification. Sanctification means the perfection of Jesus Christ manifesting itself in actual experience. If you take Abraham as a picture of sanctification, you will have to chop his life up and say—This part is sanctification, and that is not; and you will produce a false spiritual interpretation. Abraham is a picture of the life of faith, not the result of faith. He portrays for all time the ups and downs, the haphazards and the tests, the nobilities and the blunders of the perfectly actual life of faith.

(III) WHILE THE VICTORIOUS IS WORTHY. v. 21—24

Abraham renounces any advantage for himself, but he preserves the rights of those with him. We have the perfect right not to insist on our rights, it is the privilege of a Christian to waive his rights; but we do not always recognize that we must insist on those associated with us getting their rights. If they prefer to take the line of faith that we take, that is their responsibility, but we are not exonerated from seeing that they get their rights.

A STAR-HITCHED WAGON

Genesis xv. 1—6

'Be near me when my light is low,
    When the blood creeps, and the nerves prick
    And tingle; and the heart is sick,
And all the wheels of Being slow.

Be near me when the sensuous frame
    Is rack'd with pangs that conquer trust;
    And Time, a maniac scattering dust,
And Life, a Fury slinging flame.'

Tennyson

'And he believed in the Lord.' v. 6

The title represents the wildness of God's expectations. If only He had told us to hitch our wagon to a mule, we could see how it might be done; but to tell us to hitch our natural lumbering wagons to the star of Almighty God makes us wonder whether we have understood Him aright. Faith sticks to the wagon and the star; fanaticism jumps from the wagon to the star and breaks its neck. A saint is not an angel and never will be; a saint is the flesh and blood theatre in which the decrees of God are carried to successful issues. All of which means that God demands of us the doing of common things while we abide in Him.

(I) THE VISION IN THE VALLEY OF AFTERWARDS. v. 1

The meaning of the valley of afterwards is that there must be an interchange between actualities and realities, it is the successful interchange between the two that keeps the life healthy. There is no 'afterwards' to the one who lives his life mystically only; a life that produces no results is an intensely selfish life. There must be the interchange between my real standing before God and my life on the earth, i.e., my wagon must be hitched to the star, and hitched to it by faith.

43

The afterwards of success for God produces the feeling—Was it worth while? The coward fears before danger; the heroic spirit fears afterwards. It was after the victory, when Abraham went into the valley of the afterwards, that God said to him—'Fear not, Abram, I am thy shield, and thy exceeding great reward.' If you say, 'My goal is God Himself' before you have been to school, it is merely a nursery rhyme; but say it after winning a victory that tells for God, and the victory does not seem such a glorious thing after all, until you find that the goal is not a prize, but the fulfilment of a decree of God in and through you.

(II) THE VEIL ON THE VISION OF ABRAHAM. v. 2—3

Abraham is not rebellious, but he is not hilarious. He believes that Eliezer must be his heir, and he acquiesces in the purpose of God and only wants light as to the meaning of it. The phrase—'Behold, to me Thou hast given no seed' is not a murmur against God, but a pious exclamation of weakness. It is not a challenge to God, but an expression of resignation; Abraham is blaming himself for misinterpreting God— 'Excuse me for being so disappointed, Lord, but I find that all my hopes and ideas have been wrong'; but he came to find that they were not wrong.

Beware of being sorry for God's reputation in your particular case. Self-pity is Satanic; but pity for God is the betrayal of your affections. Here Abraham is in the condition not of pitying himself, but of pitying God's reputation in himself; he cannot understand how God is going to fulfil what He has said—no heir other than Eliezer, the idea of having a child must have been a misinterpretation. The veil on the vision of Abraham makes him say: It can't be done—I want an explanation as to Your meaning. When God's promise refers to fertility in mud, we must not think it refers to birds of paradise in heaven, and because we see the mud only and no sign of fertility, say we are mistaken. If any

44

promise of God that has emphatically to do with this earth and with flesh and blood people, is not being fulfilled, beware of saying—Oh well, I must have misinterpreted what God meant. We forget that we have to build in absolute confidence on God. There is nothing more heroic than to have faith in God when you can see so many better things in which to have faith. It is comparatively easy to have faith in God in a pathetic way in the starvation of things round about you, but a different matter to have faith in God after a tremendous victory has been won, and then in the aftermath that follows to think that there is to be no realization of that for which God had caused you to hope.

(III) THE VOICE AND THE VASTNESS OF ALTITUDE. v. 4--5

In this chapter we fathom the depths of all that the New Testament unfolds. Abraham the childless is to become the father of nations—How mad the promise sounds! 'And He brought him forth abroad, and said, Look now toward heaven, and tell the stars. . . . So shall thy seed be.' God points Abraham away from his wagon in the mud to the starry night, and hitches the two together by His own word. God's appeal to the stars is not to furnish proof for a doubting mind, but to provide nourishment for a faltering faith. Nature to the saint is a sacrament of God, not merely a series of facts; not symbols and signs, but the real evidence of the coming of God as a sacrament to His faithful children.

The whole discipline of the life of faith is to mix together the light of heaven and the sordid actuality of earth. Contemplation and consideration must go together, i.e., take your plan for what you do on earth from the altitude of heaven; let contemplation of the stars be mixed with what you build on earth.

In personal life despise these two things—dumps and hurry; they are worse than the devil, and are both

45

excessively culpable. Dumps is an absolute slur against God—I won't look up, I have done all I could but it is all up, and I am in despair. Hurry is the same mood expressed in an opposite way—I have no time to pray, no time to look to God or to consider anything, I must do the thing. Perspiration is mistaken for inspiration. Consequently I drive my miserable little wagon in a rut instead of hitching it to a star and pulling according to God's plan. God hitched the wagon of Abraham to the stars which He had created, by His word. In our personal lives the great solution is always found in the words of Our Lord when we have His Spirit. Jesus Christ is God Incarnate, and He makes His words spirit and life to us; our little human wagons are hitched to the star of God's sacramental purpose by the words of Jesus and in no other way. Whenever we indulge in hurry or in the dumps and refuse to pay attention to His words, we smash the connecting line and go off on our own.

(IV) THE VERACITY AND VIRTUE OF ATTITUDE. v. 6

'And he believed in the Lord.' This is the act by which Abraham goes out of himself and relies upon God for righteousness and grace. Abraham had manifested many noble qualities of heart and many virtues in his walk of faith, but he is not made righteous before God by these. The lack in Abraham is supplied through his living confidence in God. The justification of every sinner is by faith and by faith alone, and when a man walks in that faith his justification appears in his flesh and justifies God (see Psalm li. 4).

This verse is the first germ of the great doctrine of 'The Lord our Righteousness.' Righteousness must never be made to mean less than a guiltless position in the presence of justice and right. God justifies me by my supernatural faith in Him, but it is my just walk that proves Him just in saving me; if I do not walk in the life of faith, I am a slander to God.

GOOD *VERSUS* BEST

Genesis xvi. 1—6

'How the world is made for each of us!
   How all we perceive and know in it
Tends to some moment's product thus,
   When a soul declares itself—to wit,
By its fruit, the thing it does!

'Be hate that fruit or love that fruit,
   It forwards the general deed of man.
And each of the Many helps to recruit
   The life of the race by a general plan;
Each living his own, to boot.'

Browning

'She fled from her face.' v. 6

In the spiritual life we do not go from good to better,
and from better to best; because there is only One to
Whom we go, and that One is The Best, viz., God
Himself. There can be no such thing as God's second
best. We can perversely put ourselves out of God's
order into His permissive will, but that is a different
matter. In seeking the Best we soon find that our
enemy is our good things, not our bad. The things
that keep us back from God's best are not sin and
imperfection, but the things that are right and good
and noble from the natural standpoint. To discern
that the natural virtues antagonize surrender to God
is to bring our soul at once into the centre of our
greatest battlefield. Very few of us debate with the
sordid and the wrong, but we do debate with the good;
and the higher up we go in the scale of the natural
virtues, the more intense is the opposition to Jesus
Christ, which is in inverse ratio to what one would
naturally imagine (cf. Matt. xxiii. 31).

47

(I) THE FANATICISM OF SELF-DENIAL. v. 1—2

The childless state of Abraham's house was its great sorrow, and was a constant trial to Abraham's faith. Everything to do with Abraham's call was dependent upon his having seed. It is instructive to note where both Abraham and Sarah began to go wrong. They did their best to fulfil God's command, but in so doing they got out of God's order into His permissive will. The fanatical passionate desire to fulfil God's will led them into desperate error. Beware of the fanaticism of self-denial, it will lead to error lasting in its effects. When we go off on that line we become devoted to our interpretation of our destiny. Destiny is never abstract. The destiny of a human being is vested in personal relationship to God. Abraham learned this lesson later; on Mount Moriah he distinctly proved that he knew the difference between obeying what God said and obeying God Who said it. Fanaticism is sticking true to my interpretation of my destiny instead of waiting for God to make it clear. The fanatical line is—*Do* something; the test of faith lies in *not* doing. Fanaticism is always based on the highest I believe; a sordid being is never fanatical. Our Lord taught His disciples to pray—'Lead us not into temptation.' To say—'Lord, I will do whatever You tell me to do; I will stand loyal to You,' is deliberately to disobey this caution of Our Lord.

Natural impulse in a saint leads to perdition every time unless it is brought into obedience to the destiny of God, then it is turned into inspiration. It is not that impulse is wrong, but it will lead to wrong unless it is brought into obedience to the spiritual destiny of the life, and this can only be done by devotion to the One Who founds our destiny for us, Our Lord Himself. Beware of trying to forestall God's programme by your own impulse.

48

(II) THE FALSITY OF SAGACIOUS DISCERNMENT. v. 4

Abraham and Sarah both adhered to their sagacious
discernment in acting in accordance with the practice
of the time in which they lived. Beware of discerning
according to your own sagacity how God must do
some things, because it means that you dictate to
God—That word of God must be fulfilled; I cannot
allow that I have been deluded, therefore there is only
one thing left to do. That is leaning to your own
understanding instead of trusting in the Lord with all
your heart. Never say—God must do this thing. He
must not; God will fulfil His own word. You have no
business to dictate to Him, you have to remain true to
God and when His word is fulfilled, you will know He
has fulfilled it because it is a supernatural fulfilment.
Always beware of being more eager to do God's will
than God is for you to do it. The remarkable thing
about the life of Our Lord was not that He was eager
to do God's will, but that He was *obedient* to do it.
He never put His fingers across the threads of His
Father's providential order for Him and gave a tug
saying—'Now I will help You,' and pulled the thing
right out of His Father's hands. He simply obeyed,
leaving His Father's wisdom to arrange all for Him.
We rush in and say—I see what God wants and I will
do it, and we wound our own souls and injure other
lives.

(III) THE FRENZY OF SPENT DEVOTION. v. 5

Sarah's appeal in which she demands that the wrong
should be upon Abraham—'My wrong be upon thee'—
is a passionate outbreak. The whole thing is the consequence of the wrong into which Abraham has allowed
himself to be drawn. It is significant to note that both
Adam and Abraham receive the severe judgment of
God; they heeded the voice of their wives and they
had no business to. The full force of God's judgment
comes on the man, not on the woman. All through it

49

is man who is held responsible, he may escape from man's judgment but never from God's judgment ultimately. Nothing in the way of judgment is visited by God on the woman (cf. 1 Tim. ii. 14); in human judgment it is the opposite. In this case the punishment fell distinctly on Abraham, although the instigation came from the fanatical self-denial of Sarah. God never holds a woman responsible in the same way as He does a man.

(IV) THE FANATICISM OF SENSUAL DOMINION. V. 6

Sarah through her harsh treatment of Hagar evidently thrust her back into the position of a mere slave; Hagar believed that she had grown above that position, and fled. Hagar does not stand for sin, but for the natural life when it gets out of place and up against the spiritual life. Hagar and her son received real protection and blessing from God. Sin can never be in a subordinate position. My natural life must be in subordination and under the absolute control of the spiritual. The natural must be turned into the spiritual by obedience, whatever sword has to go through its heart. The natural life must be 'spiked' for the glory of God. The characteristic of the natural life is the independent passion for free dominion over itself. Immediately the natural life fights to get away, it comes into opposition. It is the *good* that hates the *best*. It is not only sin that produces the havoc in life, but the natural determination to 'boss the show' for God and everyone else.

CONTINUOUS CONVERSION

Genesis xvi. 7—16

'Lord, I have fallen again—a human clod!
Selfish I was, and heedless to offend;
Stood on my rights. Thy own child would not send
Away his shreds of nothing for the whole God!
Wretched, to thee who savest, low I bend:
Give me the power to let my rag-rights go
In the great wind that from thy gulf doth blow.

Keep me from wrath, let it seem ever so right:
My wrath will never work thy righteousness.
Up, up the hill, to the whiter than snow-shine,
Help me to climb, and dwell in pardon's light.
I must be pure as thou, or ever less
Than thy design of me—therefore incline
My heart to take men's wrongs as thou tak'st mine.'
George MacDonald

'Whence camest thou? . . . Return, . . . and submit.' vv. 8—9.

Hagar represents the natural life, she does not represent sin; sin cannot be converted. I have continually to convert the natural life into submission to the Spirit of God in me and not say—I will never do anything natural again; that is fanatical. When by the providence of God my body is brought into new conditions, I have to see that my natural life is converted to the dictates of the Spirit of God in me. Because it has been done once is no proof that it will be done again. 'Except ye be converted, and become as little children . . .' is true for all the days of the saintly life, we have continually to turn to God. The attitude of continuous conversion is the only right attitude to-

51

wards the natural life, and it is the one thing we object to. Either we say the natural is wrong and try to kill it, or else we say that the natural is all there is, and that everything natural and impulsive is right. Neither attitude is right. The hindrance in spiritual life is that we will not be continuously converted, there are 'wedges' of obstinacy where our pride spits at the throne of God and says—'I shan't; I am going to be boss.' We cannot remain boss by the sheer power of will; sooner or later our wills must yield allegiance to some force greater than their own, either God or the devil.

(I) THE ANGEL OF THE LORD AND WRECKED PASSION.
v. 7

Hagar in her helpless condition is in a fit state for the angel of the Lord to appear to her. Sarah's fanatical self-denial and vindictive spite are far from right, but they do not justify Hagar for her passionateness. I alone am responsible for the wrong I do. Hagar desired to be the mother of the seed of Abraham, but she was not to be; in her own mind she insisted on being not only the equal of Sarah but her displacer. Beware of passion that makes you reach for position, because it will end in spiritual infamy. Passion is the combination of desire and pride with a wild reach of possibility. The desire may be for a big or a little thing, but the instant result of anything done at the spur of passion lands you in a wilderness of disgust, nursing wounded pride.

The right relationship of Hagar to Sarah is to be the relationship of my natural life to the domination of the Holy Ghost. My natural life must not rule, the spiritual must rule, and it must rule over the natural life, which is represented by Hagar. I have to convert my natural life continually into submission to the Spirit of God in me, otherwise I shall produce the divorce which ends in hell.

52

(II) THE ANGEL OF THE LORD AND WOUNDED PRIDE. v. 8—9

The angel of the Lord and conscience say the same thing—Return and submit—yet they stand distinct. If the voice of God does not correspond with what conscience says, I need pay no attention to it; but when it says the same thing as conscience, I must either obey or be damned in that particular. Return from assumed responsibility and submit—to the old oppression? Yes, but without the element of passion and of pride, and the result will be according to the will of God.

Natural pride has to do with my standing before men, not before God—I shall not bow, I will make others bow to me. That is natural domination, and represents the antagonism of the natural life to the domination of the Holy Spirit. Wherever there is natural pride the Lord must inevitably be put to open shame.

(III) THE ANGEL OF THE LORD AND THE WORD OF PROMISE. v. 10—12

'The Lord hath heard thy affliction.' Throughout the Bible this is the revelation of the personal attitude of God to the miseries of the world. He is not indifferent, the cry does not go up to the ears of a deaf God.

Hagar's great desire is to be the mother of the believing children of Abraham; the angel says—No, Hagar is to be the mother of Ishmael, and Ishmael is to be blessed. The limitation of the promise is connected with the promise itself. Do not miss the point of Hagar's mistake. Hagar must be cured of the delusion that she is destined to become the mother of the believing seed of Abraham—'Cast out the bondwoman and her son': i.e. cast them out of the position they have no right to be in (*see* Gal. iv. 30).

The attitude of Our Lord towards anything to do with the natural is that of unflinching, patient sternness; He is not cruel, but He is stern, just as He was stern with His mother (John ii. 4), and just as the apostle Paul was stern with his own body (1 Cor. ix. 27).

When we are born again we enthrone Ishmael, that is, we consecrate our natural gifts and say these are the things with which God is going to do His work: they are the things God makes His servants, and I have to see that they are put in the position of servants If I put them on the throne, I start a mutiny within my own soul. The bondwoman and her child have to be cast out; the natural has to be sacrificed in order that it may be brought into perfect at-home-ness with the Spirit of God. If we make our natural life submit and obey the Holy Spirit within us, we will hasten the time for the manifestation of the sons of God (Romans viii. 21). It is the man who can rule his natural spirit that is able to take the city. It is only when we have learned to bring the natural life into perfect submission to the ruling personality of God that God dare turn His saints loose. It is of no use to turn out a lot of 'half-baked Ephraims' into unlimited power. If I enthrone natural pride or natural virtue, I am in total insubordination to God in just that particular and cannot be His son or daughter.

(IV) THE APPEARING OF THE LORD AND WAITING PATIENCE. v. 13—16

'Thou art a God that seeth.' We *see* for the first time when we do not look. We see actual things, and we say that we see them, but we never really see them until we see God; when we see God, everything becomes different. It is not the external things that are different, but a different disposition looks through the same eyes as the result of the internal surgery that has taken place. We see God, and then we see things actually as we never saw them before.

THE RESERVATIONS OF GOD

Genesis xvii. 1

'Oh, we're sunk enough here, God knows!
But not quite so sunk that moments,
Sure tho' seldom, are denied us,
When the spirit's true endowments
Stand out plainly from its false ones,
And apprise it if pursuing
Or the right way—or the wrong way,
To its triumph or undoing:

There are flashes struck from midnights,
There are fire-flames noondays kindle,
Whereby piled-up honours perish,
Whereby swollen ambitions dwindle,
While just this or that poor impulse,
Which for once had play unstifled,
Seems the sole work of a life-time
That away the rest have trifled.'

Browning

'I am the Almighty God.' v. 1

God is a perplexing Being to man because He is never in the wrong, and through the process of allowing every bit of man's wrongdoing to appear right at the time, He proves Himself right ultimately. Beware of the conception that God has to use His wits to keep Himself from being outwitted by man and the devil. God will never have more power than He has now; if He could have, He would cease to be God. Individually we may thwart God's purpose in our lives for a time, but God's purpose will be fulfilled, wherever we end. Human free will is God's sovereign work, and God not only respects it in man but He delights to posit it in him. I have perfect power not to do God's will, and I have that power by the sovereign will of God; but I can never thwart God's will ultimately. God allows ample room for man and the devil to do their worst; He allows the combination of other wills to work out to the last lap of exhaustion so that that way need never be tried again, and men will have to confess, either reluctantly or willingly, that God's purpose was right after all. And this holds true in the individual lives of God's children. I am at liberty if I choose to try every independent plan of my own, but I shall find in the end (whether too late or not is another matter), that what God said I had better do at the beginning was the right thing, if only I had listened to Him.

Every blunder Abraham made was repeated in his descendants by the inevitableness of God's providence. The consequence of doing wrong is brought out in the life of Abraham in great prominence, but the abiding truth remains the same for each one of us. It is not cause and effect, but because God is God.

(I) THE RIGOUR OF THE EVERLASTING NO. 'The Lord appeared to Abram.'

Compare Ch. xv. 1—'The word of the Lord came unto Abram *in a vision*.' God's method all through seems to be vision first and then reality. So many mistake the vision for the reality, but in between the vision and the reality there is often a deep valley of humiliation, cf. xv. 12—'Lo, an horror of great darkness fell upon him.' How often has a faithful soul been plunged into a like darkness; after the vision has come the test and the darkness. Whenever God gives a vision to a saint, He puts the saint, as it were, in the shadow of His hand, and the saint's duty is to be still and listen. Ch. xvi is an illustration of the danger of listening to good advice when it is dark instead of waiting for God to send the light (cf. Gal. i. 15—16). When God gives a vision and darkness follows, wait;

God will bring you into accordance with the vision He has given if you will wait His time. We try to do away with the supernatural in God's undertakings. Never try and help God fulfil His word. There are some things we cannot do, and that is one of them.

Never try to anticipate the actual fulfilment of a vision; you transact some business spiritually with God on your mount of transfiguration and by faith see clearly a vision of His purpose, and immediately afterwards there is nothing but blank darkness. You trust in the Lord, but you walk in darkness; the temptation is to work up enthusiasm, you have to stay on God and wait (Isaiah l. 10—11). If darkness turns to spiritual doldrums, you are to blame. When God puts the dark of 'nothing' into your experience, it is the most positive something He can give you. If you do anything now it is sure to be wrong, you have to remain in the centre of nothing, and say 'thank you' for nothing. It is a very great lesson, which few of us learn, that when God gives us nothing it is because we are inside Him, and by determining to do something we put ourselves outside Him. Abraham would not stay in the land when the famine came because there was nothing; he would not trust God for a child because there was not one. God kept giving Abraham 'nothing', i.e., Himself, and by determining to do something Abraham jumped outside God, and came to find that he was putting himself in the relationship of the Everlasting No. There are things God tells us to do without any light or illumination other than just the word of His command, and if we do not obey it is because we are independently strong enough to wriggle out of obeying. All God's commands are enablings, therefore it is a crime to be weak in His strength.

The phrase 'When Abraham was ninety years old and nine' is of immense significance. Thirteen years have rolled by in between Ch. xvi. 16 and Ch. xvii. 1.

Abraham had anticipated the purpose of God and had to pass through a long time of discipline. The act of Abraham and Sarah produced a complexity in God's plan all down the ages. So Moses had to wait forty years after his presumptuous attempt to reach his destination. Adam and Eve did the same thing, they took the 'short cut' (which is the meaning of temptation) and anticipated their destination to be *actually* what they were *potentially*—'as God' (Gen. iii. 5, R.V.), and thereby they went wrong. Our destination is to be as God, that is what we are here to become, and in Jesus Christ we do become so. Beware of estimating the temptation of a child of God to be less royal than it really is. The temptation of a child of God does not spring from selfish lust, but from a passionate desire to reach God's destination.

Abraham emerged out of this stage of discipline with one determination, viz., to let God have His way. There is no indication that he is relying on the flesh any longer, his reliance is on God alone. All self-sufficiency has been destroyed in every shape and form, there is not one common sense ray left as to how God is going to fulfil His word. God never hastens and He never tarries. He works His plans out in His own way, and we either lie like clogs on His hands or we assist Him by being as clay in the hands of the potter.

'*The Lord* appeared to Abram'—the real God now, not a vision. The knowledge of the real God is reached when my confidence is placed in God and not in His blessings. Paul takes Abraham as the type of the life of faith not of sanctification, but of a tried faith built on a real God.

(II) THE REALITY OF THE EVERLASTING YEA.

'I am God Almighty'—El Shaddai, the Father-Mother God, God proved as sufficient for everything. The wonder of El Shaddai (the power to create new things in the old world) runs through the whole kingdom of grace. Remember, Isaac was born of dead parents (Romans iv. 19). If I think I am going to produce the Son of God in myself by prayer, or obedience, or consecration, I am making exactly the same blunder that Sarah and Abraham made over Hagar. ' . . . which were born . . . not of the will of the flesh, nor of the will of man, but of God.' Immediately I realize that the thing is impossible, then God will do it. To be brought to the verge of the impossible is to be brought to the margin of the reservations of God. When God is bringing us there we indulge in sulky misbehaviour—'I don't want to go that way; I want Your blessings,' and when God asks if we have to come to the end of ourselves, we sit resigned and say—'It is all up now;' then suddenly we are in Paradise because we have come to the end of the thing God could not bring in. The Everlasting Yea is reached when we perceive that God is El Shaddai, the All-Sufficient God. There is no need so far as God is concerned for the years of silence and discipline if we will only be stupid enough to hear the everlasting No and not try to make it Yea—'Oh yes, I am going to try and make my natural virtues pleasing to God;' God says you cannot do it. God does not discard the old and create something entirely new; He creates something in the old until the old and the new are made one. To call conversion new birth is an impoverishment. Because a man who has lived in sin stops sinning, it is no sign that he is born from above. Jesus did not talk about new birth to a sinner, but to a religious man, a godly man full of rectitude; but Nicodemus worshipped God as a reminiscence, he had not the creation of El Shaddai in him. The creation of El Shaddai is what is made possible by the Lord Jesus (Gal. iv. 19).

(III) **THE REASONABLENESS OF THE EVERLASTING WAY.** 'Walk before Me.'

Abraham's faith is to be permanent, that is, he must walk continually before the eyes of the Almighty in the conscious unconsciousness of His presence. We won't walk before God because we are not confident in Him, and the proof that we are not confident in God is that occasionally we get into the sulks. If you are walking with God it is impossible to be in the sulks. Never have the idea that you have disobeyed when you know you have not, the reason you say so is because you are not walking in the permanent light of faith. Suppose Job had said—'If I were trusting in God I should not be treated like this'; he *was* trusting in God, and he *was* treated like that. Faith is not that I see God, but that I know God sees me; that is good enough for me, I will run out and play—a life of absolute freedom. Watch the spiritual sulks that arise because we want something other than God; we want God to give us something, to make us feel well, to give us wonderful insight into the Bible. That is not the attitude of a saint but of a sinner who is trying to be a saint, and who is coming to God to get things from Him. Unless we give to God the things we get from Him, they will prove our perdition.

(IV) **THE RECTITUDE OF THE EVERLASTING DAY.**

'And be perfect,' free from blame, or guiltless. Abraham was still lacking in the development of his faith and was therefore not blameless as yet. Had Abraham stayed in the land of promise, no matter though he starved to death, he would have been blameless, but he went down to Egypt and so was not blameless. We must beware lest we ignore what the old theologians called prevenient grace, that is, receiving beforehand the grace of God which will keep us worshipping Him instead of trusting in our wits. If we put moral wits in the place of mystic worship, we will go wrong. The life of Abraham does not stand for the life of a saint but for the life of the Father of the Faithful, consequently every error he committed, as well as every glorious thing he did, is recorded and traced out in its consequences through the history of his people. We are not to follow all the steps of Abraham, but to follow the steps of his faith (cf. 1 Cor. iv. 17).

We try to scrape our defects off and say—I think I am all right now. That is not walking blamelessly before God, but walking in determined opposition to faith in God. If I walk in faith in God there will be no specks to rub off; but if I don't walk in faith in God, everything is a defect and a stain, however good I am. It is a snare to continually think about defects, things which we really think should not be there. Imagine anyone who has seen himself in the light of Jesus Christ thinking of his defects! Why we are too filthy for words, and to be concerned because of the spots upon us is absurd. Leave the whole miserable thing alone; we have the sentence of death in ourselves that we should not trust in ourselves but in God, and there are no specks in God. I have determinedly to take no one seriously but God, and the first person I have to leave severely alone as being the greatest fraud I have ever known is myself. 'Oh I am sick of myself'—if you really were sick of yourself you would go to your own funeral and for ever after let God be all in all. Until you get to that point you will never have faith in God.

Beware of the thing that makes you go down before God and sway from side to side spiritually—'I don't know what to do;' then don't do anything. 'I don't see anything;' well, don't look for anything. 'I thought by this time I should see something;' if you don't, be foolish enough to trust in God. It is the height of madness from common-sense standpoints to have faith in God. Faith is not a bargain with

God—I will trust You if You give me money, but not if You don't. We have to trust in God whether He sends us money or not, whether He gives us health or not. We must have faith in God, not in His gifts. Let us walk before God and be perfect, you in your circumstances and I in mine, then we will prove ourselves true children of Abraham.

AWE

Genesis xvii. 2—14

'I faced a future all unknown,
No opening could I see,
I heard without the night wind moan,
The days were dark to me —
I cannot face it all alone
O be Thou near to me!

He has, He will, He worketh still,
In ways most wonderful.
He drew me from the miry clay,
He filled my cup quite full.
And while my heart can speak I'll tell
His love unspeakable.'

John Oxenham

'And Abram fell on his face.' **v. 3**

It is significant to note the times when Abraham did not speak to God but remained silent before Him, not sullen, but silent. Awe is just that—reverential dread and wonder. Beware of its imitation; the pose of reverential awe is the greatest cloak for unbelief. Awe is the condition of a man's spirit realizing Who God is and what He has done for him personally. Our Lord emphasizes the attitude of a child, no attitude can express such solemn awe and familiarity as that of a child. In the Apocalypse the attitude of St. John is that of an awestruck child of God.

(I) THE PERSONAL RELATION IN FAITHFULNESS. **v. 2**
The covenant with the Father of the Faithful is applicable to every man when once faith (i.e. a relationship between the individual and God) is born. We make covenants with ourselves, or with our

63

experiences, or with our transactions—I came out to the penitent form; or, I surrendered to God. That is a covenant of self-idolatry, an attempt to consecrate our earnest consecration to God. It is never a question of covenanting to keep our vows before God, but of our relationship to God Who makes the covenant with us. In the matter of salvation it is God's honour that is at stake, not our honour. Few of us have faith in God, the whole thing is a solemn vow with our religious selves. We promise that we will do what God wants; we vow that we will remain true to Him, and we solemnly mark a text to this effect; but no human being can do it. We have to steadily refuse to promise anything and give ourselves over to God's promise, flinging ourselves entirely on to Him, which is the only possible act of the faith that comes as God's gift. It is a personal relation to God's faith— 'between Me and thee.' *'Come unto Me'* said Jesus. The thing that keeps us from coming is religious self-idolatry; we will not let God make a covenant with us, we will make vows with God. Vowing means I can do it if I pledge myself to do it (cf. Exodus xix. 8). We have to stake ourselves on the truthfulness of God's character; what He does with us is a matter of indifference. Beware of trusting in your trust and see that you trust in the Lord, and you will never know you trust Him because you are taken up into His certainty.

(II) THE PROFOUND REALIZATION OF FRUITION. v. 3

'And Abram fell on his face.' This is an expression of deep humility and trustful confidence and pure joy; these are always the characteristics of faith in God. Every time you say—I feel I haven't got the witness, pack up and get out—out of the compartment of yourself and into the compartment of God, and stay there. Whenever you make a transaction with God, it is real instantly and you have the witness; when there is no witness, no humility, no confidence or joy, it is because you have made a transaction with your religious self and you say—I must wait for God's witness. That is self-idolatry; there is no trust in God in it, but just the mewling of a sick infant. The relation is to be that of a child; fling yourself clean over on to God and wash your hands of the consequences, and John xiv. 27—'My peace I give unto you'—becomes true at once. The profound realization of God makes you too unspeakably peaceful to be capable of any self-interest.

(III) THE PRECIOUS RECOGNITION OF FELLOWSHIP.
    v. 3—4

'And God talked with him.' The faith that is the creation of God's Spirit in the human soul is never private and personal. When once that faith is created we are caught up into the terrific universal purpose of God, 'Thou shalt be a father of many nations.' The Holy Spirit destroys our personal private life and turns it into a thoroughfare for God. Faith is not the means whereby we take God to ourselves for our select coterie; faith is the gift of God whereby He expresses His purposes through us. God wants to take us up into His purpose so that we no more keep for our joys 'a world within the world', but God can do with us exactly what He likes without saying—By your leave. God does not ask permission to use us any more than we ask permission to use our hands, but we have to keep in joint with God. Full power cannot be put into a machine that is out of gear. (Cf. 1 John i. 7.)

(IV) THE PROMISED ROYALTY OF FATHERHOOD. v. 4

This amazing promise is exactly expressive of the power of God and it produces moral hysterics. When it begins to dawn in my conscious life what God's purpose is, there is the laughter of the possibility of the impossible. The impossible is exactly what God does. The sure sign that we have no faith in God is that we have no faith in the supernatural. No man can believe God unless God is in him. The promises to Abraham are God all over from beginning to end. Don't only make room for God, but believe that God has room enough for you.

(v) THE PECULIAR RECOGNITION OF REGENERATION FAMILIARITY. v. 5

The new name 'Abraham' announces a new disposition, and circumcision represents the renewal of the whole into a more noble nature by the presence of a new disposition within until the two are made one (cf. Matt. v. 48). Hagar represents not the sinful but the natural, which must first go through the pain of being a willing slave and be turned into oneness with the purpose of God. The difficulty in personal life is that the natural in us says to God in spiteful irritation —I shan't; I won't go back to Sarah; I won't submit to any rule at all, I will boss the whole thing myself. But you cannot; you will either have to come to the death of the natural willingly, or be dragged there by the providential tyranny of God.

(VI) THE PHYSICAL SIGN OF SPIRITUALITY. v. 6—14

Circumcision, or sanctification which it symbolizes, is the decision to cut away all self-idolatry and abandon to God entirely. The old nature and the new have to be made one, and the sign that they are one is circumcision in the Old Testament and sanctification in the New. The point to remember is that the new creation is made by El Shaddai in the old world. When the Holy Spirit comes in the two natures are there distinctly, and they have to be amalgamated into one nature. The old has to be turned into a noble nature by the incoming of God; we are not to be fanatical and turn our noses up at the old. The new disposition is the one in which God is all. The Judaisers taught that all those who were of the direct historic seed of Abraham were all right. The Apostle John says No, it is not by physical generation but by supernatural generation (*see* John i. 12-13). Then came the spiritualizing people who denied that God had anything to do with the physical generation. The Apostle says No. Jesus Christ came that way (*see* 1 John iv. 2), which is a proof that everything that has been defiled is to be made holy through Christ. Beware of insulting God by being a pious prude instead of a pure person.

ECSTASIED

Genesis xvii. 15—27

'Though dim as yet in tint and line,
  We trace Thy picture's wise design,
  And thank Thee that our age supplies
  Its dark relief of sacrifice.
      Thy will be done!
  Strike, Thou the Master, we Thy keys,
  The anthem of the destinies!
  The minor of Thy loftier strain,
  Our hearts shall breathe the old refrain,
      Thy will be done!'   *Whittier*

'Then Abraham fell upon his face and laughed.'
v. 17

There are certain phases of the life of faith which
look so much like cant and humbug that we are apt to
grieve God's Spirit by our religious respectability in
regard to them, and ecstasy is just one of those phases.
An ecstasied man is one whose state of mind is marked
by mental alienation from his surroundings, and his
very consciousness is altered into excessive joy. These
states are open gateways for God or for the devil.
If they are worked up by thrills of our own seeking,
they are of the devil; but when they come unsought
in faithful performance of duties, they are the gateway
into direct communication with God. Ecstasy is not a
state in which to live; keep your ecstatic times dark.
You have no business to show the depths to anyone
but yourself and God.

We are all so abominably serious, so interested in
our own characters, that we refuse to behave like
Christians in the shallow concerns of life. Our safeguard is the God-given shallowness. It is the attitude
of a spiritual prig to go about with a countenance that

68

is a rebuke to others because you have the idea that they are shallower than you. Live the surface common-sense life in a common-sense way, and remember that the shallow concerns of life are as much of God as the profound concerns. It is not our devotion to God or our holiness that makes us refuse to be shallow, but our wish to impress others that we are not shallow, which is a sure sign that we are prigs. We are to be of the stamp of Our Lord and Master, and the prigs of His day called Him a glutton and a winebibber, they said He was not dealing with the profound things. Beware of the production of contempt for others by thinking that they are shallow. To be shallow is not a sign of being wicked: the ocean has a shore. The shallow amenities of life are appointed of God and are the things in which Our Lord lived, and He lived in them as the Son of God. It is easier for personal pride not to live in them. Beware of posing as a profound person; God became a Baby.

(I) THE PRINCESS OF GOD IN HUMAN EXPRESSION.
v. 15, 16

The name 'princess' is not earned by piety on the part of the woman, it is the new thing which has been created in her by faith in God. When we find unfortunate ingredients in Abraham and Sarah, and in ourselves, we have to realize that God's designations refer to what He redemptively creates in us, and not to our decorations of ourselves. The treasure is 'in earthen vessels.' A princess in God's sense is not a princess when she prides herself on her own initiative. When Our Lord says, 'the same is My sister, and mother,' note the condition of His designation, viz., 'whosoever shall *do* the will of My Father which is in heaven;' not whosoever has done the will of God once. Doing the will of God is instantaneously continuous. Am I doing the will of God *now?* Faith does not give us a feeling of eternal life upon which we draw; faith is a fountain of living water overflowing. If I keep living the life of faith then I shall be a sister of the Lord Jesus. There is only one way to live the life of faith, and that is to *live it*.

(II) THE PARADOXES OF GOD AND HUMAN EMOTION.
v. 17

This is the first time laughter is mentioned in the Bible, and the first mention of a thing in the Bible colours its meaning all the way through. Abraham's laughter had in it no intermixture of wrong. Laughter and weeping are the two intensest forms of human emotion, and these profound wells of human emotion are to be consecrated to God. The devil is never said to laugh. Laughter that is not the laughter of a heart right with God, a child heart, is terrible; the laughter of sin is as the crackling of burning thorns. Whenever the angels come to this earth they come bursting with a joy which instantly has to be stayed (cf. Luke ii. 13). This earth is like a sick chamber, and when God sends His angels here He has to say—'Now be quiet; they are so sick with sin that they cannot understand your hilarity.' Whenever the veil is lifted there is laughter and joy. These are the characteristics that belong to God and God's order of things; sombreness and gloom, oppression and depression, are the characteristics of all that does not belong to God.

The promise was so great that Abraham sank reverently upon the ground, and so paradoxical that he ecstatically laughed—'Is it to be now at this late day even as Thou didst assure me it was to be?' There was no doubt, but amazement; the thing was so completely impossible that Abraham believed it absolutely, so absolutely that his equilibrium was upset. We have all experienced ecstasy in minor degrees. Every time we have transacted business with God on His covenant and have let go entirely on God, there is no sense of merit in it, no human ingredient

70

at all, but such a complete overwhelming sense of being a creation of God's that we are transfigured by peace and joy.

(III) THE PURPOSE OF GOD AND HUMAN EXPECTATION.
   v. 18—21

Abraham was all this time contented with the supposition that Ishmael was the child of promise, but in this new revelation he receives the definite statement of God that Sarah shall bear to him the true heir, and the promise is revealed even in regard to time. Up till now there had been the mingling of doubt with Abraham's faith, he did not trust God completely because he did not see how He was going to fulfil His word (cf. Luke xxiv. 41). In v. 20 the promise is still more clearly revealed, and with this revelation God withdraws—'and God went up from Abraham'.

(IV) THE PROGRAMME OF GOD AND HUMAN EXERCISE.
   v. 22—27

These verses state how Abraham complies with the prescribed rite of circumcision. God uses circumcision (as He did the rainbow) and makes it a sign and symbol for something it never was until He made it so. Circumcision becomes with the historic people of God a real sign of the covenant with God that they are His people, but there must be an accompanying sign of our agreement with God. For instance, the physical exertion of coming to a penitent form has a more emphatic meaning than we imagine, and it is against those exertions that human nature protests—'But it is so humiliating.' Of course it is! If you sit tight against the monitions of the Holy Ghost, you will make yourself obtuse to the voice of God. The thing that keeps you back from obeying is the domination of natural human pride that will not bow to God. Salvation will never be actual until you physically commit yourself to it (Romans x. 10).

71

FRIEND OF GOD

Genesis xviii. 1—15

'Nor hope to find
A Friend but what has found a Friend in thee!—
All like the purchase; few the price will pay;
And this makes Friends such miracles below.

But since Friends grow not thick on every bough,
Nor ev'ry Friend unrotten at the core;
First on Thy Friend, delib'rate with thyself!
Pause—ponder—sift! not eager in the choice
Nor jealous of the chosen:—fixing, fix!
Judge before Friendship, then confide till death.'

Young

'Pass not, I pray Thee, from Thy servant.' v. 3

The Apostle James calls Abraham 'the Friend of God.' The foundations of friendship with God are laid in inborn qualities; Abraham has that in him now which makes it possible for him to be the friend of God. Never confound 'Saviour' with 'friend;' Our Lord said 'Ye are My friends' to His disciples, not to sinners. Friendship with God means that there is now something of the nature of God in a man on which God can base His friendship. These inborn qualities are formed in me by the incoming of the Holy Spirit, they are not there by natural generation; then as I obey the revelation granted to me, friendship with God begins, based on the new life which has been created in me. That new life has no affinities on the old lines, but only on the line of God, and is unutterably humble and holy, unsulliedly pure, and absolutely devoted to God. 'El Shaddai'—the One Who creates something *in* the old world, and transfigures it.

Friendship with God is faith in action in relation to God and to our fellow men. 'A new commandment

72

I give unto you, that ye love one another; even as I
have loved you.' I love others as God has loved me,
and I see in the ingratitude of others the ingratitude
which I have exhibited to God. The fellowship which
arises out of such a friendship is a delight to the heart
of God.

(I) THE ALTAR OF FELLOWSHIP. v. 1—5

This manifestation of God to Abraham is the most
striking sign in the old Covenant of the Incarnation.
The Incarnation in practical identification means the
manifestation of God in mortal flesh in every detail
of human life. Our Lord was not an ascetic like John
the Baptist, He was not limited, or proscribed and
fanatical. In Our Lord's life the natural and the
supernatural were reconciled, the natural was not
violently discarded. There was no ostensible preparation for the coming of the Son of God. How many
knew that Jesus was God Incarnate? (John i. 11-12.)
It was only when the surgery of events had taken
place that their eyes were opened and they knew Him
(Luke xxiv. 31). Our Lord comes in the most casual
way, and we will miss Him unless we are prepared
in our nature to discern Him. The most amazing
evidence of a man's nature being changed is the way
in which he sees God, to say 'God led me here;' 'God
spoke to me;' is an everyday occurrence to him.

The altar of fellowship means that in every occurrence of life I offer myself in devotion to God. Abraham had difficulty at first in bringing the actual
details of his life into touch with his real faith in God.
Our Lord's actual life was a continual manifestation of
His real faith in God, every detail—washing disciples'
feet, fasting, praying, marriage feasts—manifested
the altar of fellowship.

(II) THE DISCIPLINE OF FELLOWSHIP. v. 6—8

The reality of God being our Guest is the most
awful joy in the discipline of fellowship. The spirit

73

of hospitality consists in this, that in or with the stranger, we receive the Lord Himself. If Abraham could have done more for God actually than he would for any other, his fellowship with God was imperfect; but Abraham did no other for God than he would have done for a stranger, and this is the essential of readiness for God. We do our best to dress ourselves up, we put on behaviour that is not ours, moods that have nothing to do with us, all in order to offer God suitable accommodation. The only way in which we can have God as our Guest is by receiving from Him the Holy Spirit Who will turn our bodies into His house. It is not that we prepare a palace for God, but that He comes into our mortal flesh and we do our ordinary work, in an ordinary setting, amongst ordinary people, as for Him. Our Lord teaches that we have to receive those He sends as Himself (Matt. x. 40). When therefore we receive hospitality from others in His name, we have to remember that it is being offered to our Master, not to us. It is easier to receive the rebuffs and the spurnings than to receive the hospitality and welcome really offered to Our Lord. We say—'But I cannot accept this;' if we are identified with our Lord we will have to go through the humiliation of accepting things of which we feel ourselves unworthy.

Times of feasting reveal a man's master like nothing else in human life, and it is in those times that Our Lord reveals Himself to be Master. My treatment of Jesus Christ is shown in the way I eat and drink, I am either a glutton and put Jesus Christ to shame, or else I am an ascetic and refuse to have fellowship with Him in eating and drinking; but when I become a humble saint I reveal Him all the time in the ordinary common ways of life. The ordinance of the Lord's Supper is a symbol of what we should be doing all the time. It is not a memorial of One Who has gone, but of One Who is always here, 'This do in remembrance of Me'—be in such fellowship with Me that you show My death until I manifest Myself again. It is in the common things of life that evidence of the discipline of fellowship is given.

(III) THE ILLUMINATION OF FELLOWSHIP. v. 9—15

'Sarah laughed within herself.' Abraham's laughter was that of joyful faith (Ch. xvii. 17); Sarah's laughter was that of doubting little faith. Sarah had to come to the place where her faith was as active as Abraham's, where she was certain that what God had said would happen, would happen. There are times when God seems to overlook certain forms of unbelief, at the other times He brings our unbelief out suddenly into the light and makes us cringe with shame before it. It is not because He wants to show how miserable and mean we are, but because our particular form of un-faith is hindering the expression of His purpose in and through us.

A child of faith must never limit the promise of God by what seems good to him, but must give to the power of God the preference over his own reason. God never contradicts reason, He transcends it always. We 'limit the Holy One of Israel' by remembering what we have allowed Him to do for us in the past; this hinders God and grieves His Spirit. In a time of communion God brings to us a real illumination of His word and we feel thoroughly exhilarated, then we begin to bring in our 'But's'. Whenever you are severely rebuked by God for indulgence in unbelief, take it as an honour from God, because prompt obedience on your part will mean the expression of God's purpose in and through you. The things that burden us either make us laugh at their absurdity, or else make us realize that God is burdening us for His own purpose.

In v. 9-14 we have a record of the most remarkable table-talk in the world, the table-talk of God with Abraham and his wife.

GETTING THERE

Genesis xviii. 16—33

'If we with earnest effort could succeed
   To make our life one long connected Prayer,
  As lives of some perhaps have been and are:—
If—never leaving Thee—we had no need
Our wandering spirits back again to lead
   Into Thy presence, but continued there,
   Like angels standing on the highest stair
Of the sapphire throne—this were to pray indeed!
  But if distractions manifold prevail,
   And if in this we must confess we fail,
Grant us to keep at least a prompt desire,
   Continual readiness for Prayer and Praise—
An altar heaped and waiting to take fire
   With the least spark, and leap into a blaze!'

                              Trench

'And Abraham drew near, and said. . . .'

'Getting there' means coming into intimate relationship with God without impertinence or lack of reverence. The meaning of intercession is that we see what God is doing, consequently there is an intimacy between the child and the Father which is never impertinent. We must pour into the bosom of God the cares which give us pain and anxiety in order that He may solve for us, and before us, the difficulties which we cannot solve. We injure our spiritual life when we dump the whole thing down before God and say—You do it. That spirit is blind to the real union with God. We must dump ourselves down in the midst of our problems and watch God solve them for us. 'But I have no faith'—bring your problems to God and stay with Him while He solves them, then God Himself and the solution of your problems will be for ever your own. Watch the tendency to pathetic humbug in your approach to God. If we could see the floor of God's immediate presence, we would find it strewn with the 'toys' of God's children who have said—This is broken, I can't play with it any more, please give me another present. Only one in a thousand sits down in the midst of it all and says—I will watch my Father mend this. God must not be treated as a hospital for our broken 'toys', but as our Father.

(1) THE ACTUAL AND REAL IN UNION. v. 16—19

v. 16 reveals the union of vision and actual life. Abraham sees Jehovah, but he also does his duty to his guests; he does not forget the courtesy of seeing his sublime visitors on their way as if they were ordinary men. The union of the actual and the real was an habitual condition in the life of Our Lord; it is not so with us until we learn to make it so. We have a wonderful time of communion with God, then comes the spiritual pout—I have to go and clean boots, or write an essay! In Our Lord's life there was no divorce between the actual and the real, He never gave Himself 'continually to prayer.' Beware of the tendency that makes you wish that God would pretend you are someone special, it is a childish make-believe, standing on spiritual tiptoe to look as big as God—others can do this and that, but I must give myself to prayer. The great secret of the obedient life of faith is that the actual conditions of bodily life are transfigured by real communion with God.

'Shall I hide from Abraham that which I do?' Notice the communing of God with Himself before He gives the revelation to Abraham. God cannot reveal Himself to anyone; the revelations of God are determined by the condition of individual character (cf. Psalm xviii. 24-26); God takes up the man who is

77

worthy to be the recipient of a revelation. Abraham by his own obedience was fitted to receive the revelation, and this is recognized by God when He brings him into union with Himself, not into absorption, but into complete union.

(II) THE AWFUL RECKONING ULTIMATELY. v. 20—22

The moral demand is for the punishment of sin. Every grain of sand cries out for its punishment (cf. Genesis iv. 10). Human beings do not echo the cry, only one or two echo it in intercession, and the cry of Nature is joined by the man who knows God.

'I will know.' This is the introduction of the final decision. It must become evident in the last trial whether the limit of the long-suffering patience of God has been reached. v. 22. 'And the men . . .' must be connected with Ch. xix 1. They were two angels who accompanied Jehovah, and in the form of men they depart to introduce the final test; they depart, but Abraham stands 'yet before the Lord'.

(III) THE APPEALING REVERENCE TO THE UTTERMOST. v. 23—33

There is no impertinence in Abraham's attitude, only profound humility and intensest intimacy. Abraham is not questioning God, but bringing himself to see how God will solve the matter. God allows Abraham to come out with his full intercession until Abraham begins to grasp the essential conditions by which God governs all things. Abraham goes on from step to step, and Jehovah grants him step by step, without once going before his request. The stopping point is reached by reason of the fact that Abraham was in complete communion with God throughout the progress of his intercession. After the final test prayer is impossible (cf. 1 John v. 16).

By means of intercession we understand more and more the way God solves the problems produced in our minds by the conflict of actual facts and our real faith in God. Whenever temptations contend in our minds, and things meet us in the providence of God which seem to involve a contradiction of what we believe, let the conviction of God's righteousness remain unshaken.

It is an insult to sink before God and say 'Thy will be done' when there has been no intercession. That is the prayer of impertinent unbelief—There is no use in praying, God does whatever He chooses. The saying of 'Thy will be done' is born of the most intimate relationship to God whereby I talk to Him freely. There is in this prayer of Abraham a distinction between the begging which knows no limit and the prayer which is conscious that there are limits set by the holy character of God. Repetition in intercessory importunity is not bargaining, but the joyous insistence of prayer.

The nearer Abraham came to God in his intercession the more he recognized his entire unworthiness—'Behold now, I have taken upon me to speak unto the Lord, which am but dust and ashes.' Genuine unworthiness is never shy before God any more than a child is shy before his mother. A child of God is conscious only of his entire dependence upon God.

In the beginning of our spiritual life our prayers are not of faith but of fretfulness. But when you get into the inner place I defy you to go on praying for yourself, it never occurs to you to do so because you are brought into relationship with God Who makes your spirit partake of His own. Whenever Our Lord spoke of importunity in intercession it was never for ourselves but for others. When by imperceptible degrees we stop praying for ourselves, we are 'getting there'. Prayer is the supreme activity of all that is noblest in our personality, and the essential nature of prayer is faith.

SCARCELY SAVED

Genesis xix. 1—29

'Better in bitterest agony to lie,
  Before Thy throne,
Than through much increase to be lifted up on high,
  And stand alone.

Yet best—the need that broke me at Thy feet,
  In voiceless prayer,
And cast my chastened heart, a sacrifice complete,
  Upon Thy care.'

John Oxenham

'Escape for thy life.' v. 17.

It is such chapters as these that enable us to understand the essential nature of God's Redemption.

(1) PREPARED BY GRACIOUS EXPERIENCES. v. 1—3

The manifestation which was given to Lot corresponds to that given to Abraham (*see* ch. xviii. 2). Lot was not a noble man of God like Abraham, but the fact that he bowed himself to the ground before the angels shows that he retained the power to know when God was near. In comparison with his generation, Lot was righteous, and his contact with Abraham made his manners similar to Abraham's. This preparation by gracious experiences occurs in our personal lives, and such experiences should be cherished for they enable us to do the right thing when we might otherwise do wrong. Beware of not heeding the angel of God in whatever form he comes to you.

'They entered into his house.' The entrance of God into a house does not secure anything, but reveals that there is something there with which God has affinity. It is never our merit God looks at but our

80

faith. If there is only one strand of faith amongst all the corruption within us, God will take hold of that one strand.

After every temptation notice where your affinities lie. If you have gone through the temptation successfully, your affinities will be with the highest and purest (cf. Matt. iv. 11); but if you have not the same affinity with the highest, it is a sign that you have become blunted in your spiritual susceptibilities. The seal of doom in a man is that he cannot believe in purity, and this can only be accounted for by an internal twist; no man gets there easily. What is true in individual lives has become appallingly true in Sodom.

God has given us a precious gift in that looking at other Christians we see not them but the Lord. If you see only where others are *not* the Lord, it is you who are wrong, not they; you have lost the bloom of spirit which keeps you in touch with Jesus Christ. If I cannot see God in others, it is because He is not in me. If I get on my moral high horse and say it is they who are wrong, I become that last of all spiritual iniquities, a suspicious person, a spiritual devil dressed up as a Christian. Beware of mistaking suspicion for discernment, it is the biggest misunderstanding that ever twisted Christian humility into Pharisaism. When I see in others things that are not of God, it is because the Spirit of God has revealed to me my own meanness and badness; when I am put right with God on the basis of His Redemption and see those things in others, it is in order that God may restore them through my intercession. Be careful never to lose the bloom of your spiritual susceptibilities.

(II) PROPOSALS OF GREAT EVIL. v. 4

The history of Sodom reveals that sin is the beginning of the most appalling corruption. Always distinguish between what we are apt to call sin and what the Bible calls sin. The Bible does not call the corruption of Sodom sin; sin is a disposition, not a deed; the corruption of Sodom is the criminal result of sin. It is because this distinction has been lost sight of that pseudo-evangelical preaching has been to the effect that only moral blackguards can be saved. When Our Lord faced men not guilty of moral black-guardism, but worthy, upright men, He did not deal with them in the way He did with sinners; He seemed to be infinitely sterner with the Pharisees than with the publicans (*see* Matt. xxi. 31). He looked at something we do not see, viz., the disposition.

Lot was the only one who stood as a representative of God in Sodom, and while he was free from the abominations of Sodom, he was not far from its worldly mind. His was the doubting heart which soon turns to double ways. Lot's position arises from having borrowed most of his piety (Genesis xii. 4). Weak faith chooses the visible things instead of enduring as seeing Him Who is invisible, and slowly and surely such faith settles down between mammon and righteousness. In the supreme test Lot trusted his wits; Abraham worshipped and waited.

(III) PERILS OF GRIEVOUS EMOTION. v. 5—9

In the history of Sodom independence of God reaches the limit of blasphemy. The way to get there in personal life is to indulge in sentimental spirituality. If you indulge in a spiritual sentiment you do not intend to obey, the exact opposite of that emotion will come in its wake. Beware of panic, because panic always advocates doing wrong that right may result. In fact, the tendency to *do* instead of to devote one's self to God, is nearly always the sign of a smudged purity of relationship to God.

(IV) PERFORMANCE OF GOD'S ENDS. v. 10—29

Abraham standing alone with God is the key to the rescue of Lot and his family, out they come whether they like it or not. The angels are insistent in answer to Abraham's intercession (*see* v. 16). Yet Lot was rescued with the greatest difficulty because of his vacillation. Vacillation in a crisis is the sign of an unabandoned nature. An abandoned nature never can vacillate because there is nothing to weigh; such a nature is completely abandoned to another. Lot's fear was culpable because it was indicative of a stultified judgment.

See to it that you do not profane the holiness of God by refusing to abandon yourself away from your experience of what He has done for you to God Himself. Whenever you do not come in contact with God for yourself, you will begin to watch your own whiteness—I dare not say this or do that. It is a cabined, confined life and when difficulties come like a wall of fire, God has to come and rescue you; and He does it by means of intercession on the part of some one else. Beware of accepting the blessings and visions of God as an indication of your goodness and not of the mercy and purpose of God—'the Lord being merciful unto him'.

WRECKED IN HARBOUR

Genesis xix. 30—38

'A Chequer-Board of mingled Light and Shade?
And We the Pieces on it deftly laid?
Moved and removed, without a word to say,
By the Same Hand that Board and Pieces made?

No Pieces we in any Fateful Game,
Nor free to shift on Destiny the blame;
Each Soul doth tend its own immortal flame,
Fans it to Heaven, or smothers it in shame.'

John Oxenham

'And he dwelt in a cave.' v. 30.

The phrase 'wrecked in harbour' describes the character that has gone through great storms and has made the harbour, and yet is wrecked as the result of an inward, persisting defect.

> 'I am very sorry for the failures at Christchurch of which you tell. I suspect that cleverness was at the bottom of the failure, for it is a character of mind the exercise of which is so instantly and pleasantly rewarded, that the temptation to cultivate it is always present.'
>
> *Sir James Paget in a letter to his son*

Spiritual cleverness is the cause of much of our failure. We may not have much mental cleverness, but some of us are dexterously clever spiritually. We have so many memories of the times when God came in and did the thing that we determinedly 'loaf' on God—only we call it 'relying on the Holy Ghost.' There are times when God does give real spiritual insight and times when He does not, and if between the times of inspiration you do not work

84

but 'loaf', you are leading up to tremendous failure one day. The moments of light and inspiration are an indication of the standard which we must work to keep up. If between the times of inspiration we refuse to practise, we shall fail spiritually exactly where Paget's son failed intellectually. He failed because he trusted to the clever moments of his genius, and we fail because we trust to the moments of spiritual cleverness.

(I) THE NATURAL HISTORY OF THE PRUDENCE PERIL

The prudence which appears in the life of Abraham as sinful prudence (e.g., ch. xii. 10) appears again in the lives of his kindred, and is the persisting defect in the character of Lot. No man can do things and leave them with himself. He may not see the result, but he will have to answer for it generations after. The prudence peril is traceable first of all in Adam, then in Noah, then in Abraham, and right on to the end of the chapter until it becomes the most dominant characteristic of Israel and Judah. The terror of the prudence peril is that it can end in such a deed as this. These things are written for our instruction. 'But I never could do such things.' What any man has ever done, any man can do if he does not watch.

The error is putting prudence in competition with God's will, weighing *pros* and *cons* before God when He has spoken. Always beware when you want other people to commend the decision you have made, because it is an indication that you have trusted your wits instead of worshipping God. If you say 'But I can prove I was right,' you may be sure you are wrong, because you have to use your ingenuity to prove you are right. When you act in faith in God it is not logical proof that you are right that matters, but the certainty of the Divine approval, and this keeps you from seeking the approval of others. We have to watch that we use our wits to assist us in worshipping God and carrying out His will, not in carrying out our own will and then asking God very piously to bless the concoction. Put communion with God on the throne, and then ask God to direct your common sense to choose according to His will. Worship first and wits after.

(II) THE NATURAL HISTORY OF PANIC PERVERSITY

Sensual passion always follows spent panic. It is easy to fall into the sins of the flesh when once the ideals of life lose their power. All you have to do is to get into a panic on any line, and you will be as perverse as can be because you have committed a sin against your own nature. Not only so, but you have given an opportunity to the devil over your body. There was an entire absence of panic in the life of Our Lord, consequently nothing of the nature of perversity. Notice how Our Lord continually curbed Peter on the line of impulse, because impulse is apt to lead to panic, and anything of the nature of panic opens the door to perversity and sensuality. A saint has no right to give way to a panic of nerves, it is a deliberate giving way and has to be hauled up instantly. When we give way to a panic of nerves we give the temple of the Holy Ghost over to the devil. Beware of the 'panickiness' which takes the form of hysteria, because on the borders of hysteria lurk all the demons that can possess human nature. Never sympathize with anyone who is giving way to hysteria; if you do, you aid and abet Satan in thrusting the temple of the Holy Ghost into the clutches of the devil.

Never allow an emotion which you know you dare not carry out on its own level; grip it on the threshold of your mind in a vice of blood and allow it no more way. Few of us realize the power we have of doing this. I am a criminal in the sight of God for allowing an emotion with regard to anyone which I know I dare not carry out on its logical level. If once we got hold of the psychological law that an emotion not carried out on its legitimate level will react on a lower level, it would bring the wind of rugged reality into devotional meetings. It is possible to step from devotion to God into a moral cesspool in one second, and we are to blame before God for not knowing these things. God's word is as rugged and unvarnished as can be on this line, and it is the cunning and abominable nonsense of what is called good taste that prevents these things being stated. I have no business to allow false emotions before God, emotions that are not 'me' at all, and that I have not the remotest intention of carrying out. Our Lord requires not only chastity of body, He requires chastity of thought.

> 'The law that every extraordinary expansion or satisfaction of heart or brain or will is paid for, paid for inevitably without the possibility of putting off or transferring the payment, is one of the truths about which no human being with a soul a little above the brute has the slightest doubt. . . . It is an eternal and immutable verity and the soul of man is a witness to it.'

> *'The Law of Nemesis'* (*Prof. Saintsbury*)

PHILISTINISM

Genesis xx. 1—7

'When the powers of hell prevail
　　O'er our weakness and unfitness,
Could we lift the fleshly veil,
　　Could we for a moment witness
　　　　Those unnumbered hosts that stand
　　　　Calm and bright on either hand—
Oh! what joyful hope would cheer!
　　Oh! what faith serene would guide us!
Great may be the danger near,
　　Greater are the friends beside us.'

'And Abraham journeyed . . . and sojourned in Gerar.' v. 1.

The term 'Philistinism' owes its popularity to Matthew Arnold and is used to-day in reference to uncultured people. It is used here because this is the first meeting of the house of Abraham with the Philistines, and also because at this stage Abraham lapsed into uncultured confidence in himself and into compromise with spiritually uncultured people. To say 'I can't understand how Abraham could do it' is self-deception. If you will look inside your own heart, provided you do not love yourself too much, you will never say such a thing. We have to be careful lest we blind ourselves by putting up our own standards instead of looking at the standard God puts up. If we put a saint up as a standard, we blind ourselves to ourselves; it is personal vanity makes us do it. When we put God's standard up, viz., Himself, there is no room for personal vanity. It is self-deception to say—'Because I am saved and sanctified, therefore all I do is sure to be right.' As long as I establish myself amongst people who agree with me and am consciously 'bigger' than them all, it is easy to be complacent; but when circumstances oust me out amongst another set of people who do not accept my standards, my complacency is upset and I am nowhere. The grace of God makes us honest with ourselves. We must be humorous enough to see the shallow tricks we all have, no matter what our profession of Christianity. We are so altogether perverse that God Almighty had to come and save us! Whenever we forget this and begin to set up little standards of our own, imbedded in some favourite saint, we are sure to go wrong. We have to get rid of all notions about ourselves and our own standards, and keep in front what God puts in front, viz., Our Lord Himself, then we will not be tempted to delusion about ourselves. Our eye must be on God, not on ourselves.

(I) THE DISPOSITION OF REACTION. v. 1

When the Bible records facts of experience, look in your own experience for the answer; when the Bible reveals standards of revelation, look to God, not to experience.

The reaction from a state of great spiritual excitement is revealed in Abraham as well as in Lot, and as on a former occasion (*see* Ch. xii. 10) Abraham decides to change his residence—'and he sojourned in Gerar.' If we bring the light of experience to this reaction on the part of Abraham, we shall understand how even such a believer as he fell the second time into the same sin. We are apt to say—'I won't do that thing again now that God has warned me.' But you will, you will do it as certainly as Abraham did if you trust to your vows instead of to God. The one thing to do is to look steadfastly to God. Always beware when you are perfectly certain you are right, so certain that you do not dream of asking God's counsel. God never puts the judgment with our wits, but entirely with Himself, consequently we must never depend on our moral judgment or our intellec-

89

tual discernment, or on our sense of right and justice. All these are right in themselves but not right in us, we can only be right as we remain absolutely confident in God. When we realize that we have repeated a sin, the danger is to lie down in the mud and refuse to get up. There is no refuge in vowing or in praying, but only in one place, in absolute confidence in God. The child attitude is the only right one.

(II) THE DISCRETION OF REASON. v. 2

Judged from every standpoint, it would seem the right thing for Abraham to get away from the blasted country of Sodom and go to Gerar. It was not wrong from any standpoint, it was the act of a wise, sensible, reasoning man of God; but Abraham was not God's man in going because immediately he goes God rebukes him. In going to Gerar, as in going down to Egypt, Abraham thought he was justified, but in each case an entirely different thing happens from what he intended, viz., Sarah is taken from him. Whenever we bring in our ordinary wisdom as a factor of decision on any point, we are 'out of it', not morally or with human beings (it will end with a wrong relation to human beings ultimately), but our relationship to God is injured. Abraham had no notion that he was doing wrong to Abimelech, but the record proves that he did, and also that he injured his relationship to God as a faithful soul. Beware of being other than a simple child of God. The only safeguard is dependence upon God, not on godly decisions.

Beware whenever your logical moral right puts you in a wrong relation to God. 'If God will only prove that my right is right' —it is the one thing over which we are stubbornly jealous of God. 'I know I am right,' we say, and it has to be proved to us that from the standpoint of the Holy Ghost we are wrong. If I can prove to my own mind that I am right, by that very act I am wrong in disposition towards God.

(III) THE DREAM OF REALIZATION. v. 3

The fact that God makes good come out of my wrong does not make my wrong any better, I have simply utilized God's permissive will to go in a circle when I should have gone straight. There are times when you see what God wants and you begin to obey with the simple direct obedience of a child; then comes the 'choppy waters' of friends' advice or of considerations of yourself, and for a while you wobble because you have become discreet and shrewd and wise, instead of being a child of God. Then when after the passing of days, or longer, according to your stubbornness, God brings you out of all the turmoil, the devil comes and says it was a good thing after all. It was not, it was a bad thing. You prevented God's order being worked out directly through you, and He had to allow you to go in a circle and only brought you back after having grieved you through with sorrows.

Beware of justifying yourself when God alone is the justifier. If ever I can justify myself, I make God unjust. If I am right and morally based in all I do and say, I do not need a Saviour, and God is not justified in the extravagant waste of sending Jesus Christ to die for me. If God judges me a sinner who needs saving, and I can prove that I am just, I make God unjust (cf. Psalm li. 4). Every kind of upholding I give to myself, whether I be saint or sinner, is a blow in the face of God, and is a proof that I am on the wrong basis. If in any detail I take the justice of God and make it mean my own justice, I thereby prove God to be unjust. This is part of the mystery of godliness and can only be understood by the intuition of faith (Matt. xi. 25).

(IV) THE DILEMMA OF RECTITUDE. v. 4—7

God stepped in and delivered Abimelech from committing sin because of His sheer mercy—'I also withheld thee from sinning against Me.' There is a difference between deliverance from sin by God's sovereign act, which is an occasion for praise, and the defiance of sin by personal integrity, which tells in the building up of character. There are times in personal life when God by His sovereign act prevented us from committing sin, and when we look back and see how He preserved us, the danger is to say it must have been because of our innocence. No, it was of the mercy of God.

We have to learn to utilize a right reliance on circumstances in the spiritual domain, to discern that it is God Who engineers circumstances. Abraham refused to see this, and every now and again he stepped in and engineered circumstances for himself, and every time he did this, he upset everything. Reverent humility and moral pride are ultimately brought out very clearly—the former in Abraham and the latter in Abimelech. The believer in his weakness is exalted above the man of the world in his strength.

HUMILIATION

Genesis xx. 8—18

'Sink in thou blessèd sign!
Pass all my spirit through
And sever with thy sacred touch
The hollow from the true.

Through my heart's very ground
Thy ploughshare must be driven,
Till all are better loved than self,
And yet less loved than heaven.'

'And Abraham said, Because . . .' v. 11

Humiliation and humility must not be confounded. Humility can never be humiliated. To be humiliated means to be lowered in condition. The word as applied to our Lord has no reference whatever to His personal calibre, but to the lowering of His external form from *being in the form of God* to *taking the form of a servant.* Humiliation as applied to us means a lowering of condition in the sense of being mortified. Whenever we pride ourselves on anything as being of real acceptance to God and realize that He absolutely ignores that thing, we will experience the ghastly humbling of humiliation.

(I) THE HUMILITY AND HONOUR OF ABIMELECH. v. 8—10

Abimelech's true humility is revealed in the way he humbles himself in communicating the events of his dream to his courtiers, he deliberately makes known before his whole court the compromising position he is in. Verse 8 describes the intense publicity of his confession, and v. 9-11 his rigorous, yet not vindictive talk with Abraham—although there is stinging irony in what he says to Sarah (v. 16).

93

In nine cases out of ten, reserve is simply personal pride, which will turn to insolence or iniquity at a moment's notice. One of the most delicate issues in the history of the human soul is that of concealing what ought to be made known and of making known what ought to be concealed. When concealing is a great relief, question it; when revealing is a great relief, question it. The only guiding factor is obedience to the highest we know. The wriggling we indulge in to escape from being humiliated prevents our being right with God. For instance, you have a wrong attitude of mind towards another, and the Spirit of God tells you to put it right between yourself and that one (cf. Matt. v. 24), and you say—No, I will put it right between myself and God. You cannot do it; it is impossible. Instead of deliberately obeying God, irrespective of what it costs, we use the trick of prayer to cover our own cowardice. It is a very subtle subterfuge to prevent ourselves being humiliated, but God will bring us into a place of humiliation externally, and others will see we are humiliated. If, on the other hand, there is something between yourself and God, and you feel it would be an enormous relief to tell someone else about it, *don't*. 'Immediately I conferred not with flesh and blood.' It is never a question of giving an explanation to someone else, but of maintaining obedience to the highest we know at all costs.

Personal misconduct will never bring bondage on others unless the misconduct springs from an independent attitude of mind towards God. Wrong doing on the part of any student here will never interfere with the atmosphere unless along with the misconduct there is a deliberate defiance of mind against God, then the whole atmosphere of the College will be charged with antagonism, and the antagonism will last as long as that one remains at 'loggerheads' with God spiritually. It is not wrong doing but a wrong

94

attitude of mind towards God spiritually that damages the atmosphere.

It was independence of God on the part of Abraham that brought the trouble on the house of Abimelech. Abraham repeated the mistake of a former occasion because of a wrong attitude to God; he was so wrong that he thought he was doing right. Abimelech had reason to complain of the conduct of Abraham in the same way that Pharaoh had reason to complain of it (cf. Ch. xii. 13-20), and Abimelech does not shrink from declaring his injured sense of truth and justice. Imagine the humiliation it would be to Abraham when he realized what he had done.

(II) THE HUMILIATION AND HONOUR OF ABRAHAM. v. 11—18

The way in which Abraham offers his apologies reveals clearly that he was ashamed. The fear of man which had determined him earlier (Ch. xii. 11—13) was awakened afresh in him by what he had so recently seen in Sodom, and he was suspicious of human nature everywhere—'Because I thought surely the fear of God is not in this place.' Abraham ashamedly explains his motive and gives his explanation for his equivocation. In v. 12 he explains that what he said of Sarah was not untrue, but he also indicates that his reason for saying she was his sister has deservedly brought him into humiliation. There was none of the sneakish element in Abraham as there was in Jacob, his reason for denying his wife was that through her God had promised him a child, and he was trying to guard her for God.

We are always in danger of mistaking personal predilections for Christian perfection, and we have to learn to take the veil off our moral quirks. Over and over again it works like this: we begin to be cunning and think—Now, if I am not careful that man will utilize my position for his own purposes. The real reason we say it is that we do not like that particular man and imagine therefore that God does not like him either. Or else it works in this way: when someone whom we like comes, we say—Oh yes, that is of God's order; but I can't be bothered with those other people, I do not think God guided them to come. It is the same old trick, and we have to be excessively careful that we do not lean to our own understanding and try to conserve God's order in our way instead of allowing God to conserve His order in His own way.

There was never any element of fear or cunning or diplomacy in Our Lord in any shape or form. Our Lord was never suspicious of anyone; yet He trusted no one saving His Father, consequently He was never vindictive, nor was He ever humiliated. It is only possible to be humiliated when we are serving our own pride.

Abraham's defects are clear and his sins obvious, but his nobility is extraordinary. Abraham is never presented as a saint or as a type of sanctification. Phases of his life may be used to present these, but Abraham himself is the type of the life of faith in its failures and in its successes. Sanctification is not something Our Lord does in me; sanctification is *Himself* in me. 'Of Him are ye in Christ Jesus, who is made unto us . . . sanctification' (1 Cor. i. 30).

GOD IS GOOD

Genesis xxi. 1—8

'Never to be again! But many more of the kind
As good, nay, better perchance: is this your comfort to
   me?
To me, who must be saved because I cling with my
   mind
To the same, same self, same love, same God: ay, what
   was, shall be.

There shall never be one lost good! What was, shall
   live as before;
The evil is null, is nought, is silence implying sound;
What was good shall be good, with, for evil, so much
   good more;
On the earth the broken arcs; in the heaven, a perfect
   round.'   *Browning*

'God hath made me to laugh.' v. 6

One of the greatest demands of God on the human
spirit is to believe that God is good when His providence seems to prohibit the fulfilment of what He
has promised. The one character in the Bible who
sustains this strain grandly is Abraham. Paul in
summing up the life of Abraham points to it as his
greatest quality—'Abraham believed God.'

(1) GOD'S PERFORMANCE OF HIS OWN PROMISE. v. 1
No one can fulfil a promise but the one who made it.
These words contain the whole autobiography of the
godly ups and downs of the life of faith. During the
years when everything seemed to contradict the
fulfilment of the promise, Abraham continually forgot
this fundamental fact and tried to help God fulfil it.

God alone can fulfil His promise, and we have to come to the place of perfect reliance upon God (cf. 1 Thess. v. 23—24).

'The Lord visited Sarah as He had said, and the Lord did unto Sarah as He had spoken.' God visits the believer with the word of promise and visits him again with the word of fulfilment. Abraham endured for twenty-five years without any sign of fulfilment. The majority of us know nothing about waiting, we don't wait, we endure. Waiting means that we go on in the perfect certainty of God's goodness—no dumps or fear. The attitude of the human heart towards God Who promises should be to give Him credit for being as honest as He ought to be, and then to go on in the actual life as if no promise had been made. That is faithful waiting.

(II) GOD'S PRESENTATION OF HIS OWN PERFORMANCE.
v. 2

The presentation of God's performance here is in the actual details of the birth of an ordinary child, extraordinary only to the eye of faith. We come to God not with faith in His goodness but with a conception of our own, and we look for God to come to us in that way. God cannot come to me in my way, He can only come in His own way—in ways man would never dream of looking for Him. In the Incarnation the Eternal God was so majestically small that He was not detected, the world never saw Him. And this is true in regard to us, God is so insignificant providentially, that we never see Him. We cry out—'Oh God, I wish You would come to me,' when He is there all the time, and suddenly we see Him and say 'Surely the Lord is in this place; and I knew it not.' We looked for desolation and anguish, and instead there is the laughter and hilarity of realizing that we see God. This astonishment at the performance of God is brought out over and over again until we learn to be humiliated at our despicable disbelief. 'I don't know what I am going to do after Easter'—But I thought you knew God! Have all these days and weeks gone by and has God shown you nothing? Your anxiety proves that you do not believe in the goodness of God an atom, and it postpones the time of His performance.

(III) GOD'S PROGRAMME FOR HIS PROGENY. v. 3—8

What Abraham did for his son was in accordance with God's programme for him, not according to Abraham's ways for him (cf. Prov. xxii. 6). God has a distinct programme for every child born into this world, legitimately or illegitimately. If the programme is unheeded, the reason is that parents do not care about God's programme being fulfilled, but it will be fulfilled all the same. In spiritual matters be careful to note God's programme for His progeny in you. Is the Son of God formed in me? Have I heard God's promise about Him? He 'shall be called the Son of God' (Luke i. 35), that is, He has nothing to do with my natural abilities. There is no relation between the promise of God for the life He forms in us by regeneration and our personal private ambitions, those ambitions are completely transfigured. I have to heed the promise of God for my child, be it a child of nature or of grace, and see that I do not try and make God's gift fulfil my own ends. If I do, I become cruel in my judgment of God and God has to be very severe with me.

Suppose that God sees fit to put you into desolation when He begins the forming of His Son in you, what does it matter to you, and what ought it to matter? God's programme was to look after Sarah only until the child of His promise was born, and all He is after in you and me is the forming of His Son in us. When He drives the sword through the natural, we begin to whine and say 'Oh, I can't go through that', but we must go through it. If we refuse to make our natural life obedient to the Son of God in us, the Son of God will be put to death in us. We have to put on the new man in our human nature to fit the life of the Son of God in us, and see that in the outer courts of our bodily lives we conduct our life for Him.

'God hath made me to laugh.' Sarah's hilarity is the joy of God sounding through the upset equilibrium of a mind that scarcely expected the promise to be fulfilled. The son of Sarah is himself a type of the Son of Mary, and in each case the promise is limited through a particular woman, and through an apparently impossible, yet actual birth. Fancy making everything depend on that haughty, inclined-to-be-unstable, not amazingly-superb-in-rectitude Sarah! How haphazard God seems, not sometimes but always. God's ways turn man's thinking upside down.

v. 7 is indicative of the amazement that comes when God's promise is fulfilled. What is known as the dark side of Christian experience is not really Christian experience at all, it is God putting the rot of sacramental death through the natural virtues in order to produce something in keeping with His Son, and all our whining and misery ought to be the laughter of Sarah —Now I see what God wants! Instead of that, we moon in corners and gloom before God, and say 'I am afraid I am not sanctified.' If you fight against the desolation, you will kill the life of God in you; yield to it, and God's fulfilment will amaze you. It is in the periods of desolation that the sickly pietists talk about 'What I am suffering!' They are in the initial stages and have not begun to realize God's purpose. God is working out the manifestation of the fulfilment of His promise, and when it is fulfilled there is never any thought of self or of self-consideration anywhere.

WHICH?

'Profit?—Loss?
Who shall declare this good—that ill?
When good and ill so intertwine
But to fulfil the vast design
Of an Omniscient Will?—
When seeming gain but turns to loss,—
When earthly treasure proves but dross,—
And what seemed loss but turns again
To high, eternal gain?'

John Oxenham

'And God said, Let it not be grievous in thy sight.'
v. 12

The dilemmas of our personal life with God are few if we obey and many if we are wilful. Spiritually the dilemma arises from the disinclination for discipline; every time I refuse to discipline my natural self, I become less and less of a person and more and more of an independent, impertinent individual. Individuality is the characteristic of the natural man; personality is the characteristic of the spiritual man. That is why Our Lord can never be defined in terms of individuality, but only in terms of personality. Individuality is the characteristic of the child, it is the husk of the personal life. It is all 'elbows', it separates and isolates; personality can merge and be blended. The shell of individuality is God's created covering for the protection of the personal life, but individuality must go in order that the personal life may be brought out into fellowship with God—'that they may be one, even as We are one.'

Sarah is full of indignation when she sees the mocking of Ishmael, and begs Abraham to 'cast out this bondwoman and her son.' God tells Abraham to hearken to what Sarah says, and Ishmael is cast out. We have to remember, however, that Sarah gave Hagar to Abraham to be his wife; we always become anxious when we take our own self-chosen ways. In the Epistle to the Galatians the Apostle Paul makes his great revelation regarding that which was 'born after the flesh' and that which was 'born after the Spirit.' He is dealing not with sin, but with the relationship between the natural and the spiritual. The natural must be disciplined and turned into the spiritual by sacrifice (cf. Gal. v. 24), otherwise it will produce a tremendous divorce in the life. Why did God make it necessary for the natural to be sacrificed to the spiritual? God did not. God's order was that the natural should be transformed into the spiritual by obedience; sin made it necessary for the natural to be sacrificed to the spiritual, and that after sanctification, remember. We have the idea that sanctification means deliverance from sin only; it means much more, it means that we start on a life of discipline such as nine out of every ten of us will have nothing to do with.

The offence of the natural is its robust ridicule of the spiritual, and if the natural is not 'cast out' it will not only perish itself but will lead the whole personal life astray. 'I was not disciplined when I was a child.' You must discipline yourself now, if you do not, you will ruin your life for God. If the natural is not sacrificed to the spiritual by me, not by God, it will mock at the life of the Son of God in me and produce a continual 'swither', which is always the result of an undisciplined nature. Instead of 'I can't', say '*I won't*', and you have it exactly, it is the Ishmael jeer. People go wrong spiritually because they stubbornly refuse to discipline themselves physically, mentally or in any way, and after a while they become that most contemptible and objectionable thing, a petted man or woman, and their own greatest cause of suffering. There is no suffering to equal the suffering of self-love arising from independent individuality which refuses to submit either to God or to its nobler self.

(II) THE OFFERING OF THE NATURAL. v. 11—13

The casting out of the bondwoman and her son was necessary not only for the line of promise but for the welfare of Ishmael himself. All the problems regarding civilization and organization and the natural virtues arise along this line. If I put the civilized organization to which I belong, or my natural virtues, on the throne, they will make a mock of the Son of God Who is formed in me. These things are the outcome of the natural life and I have to resolutely put them under, not because they are wrong, but because they are individual protests against the life of the Son of God in me. The natural life is not spiritual, it can only be made spiritual by deliberately casting it out and making it the slave instead of the ruler. My business is to make independent individuality conform to the Son of God in me by severity. We are apt to deify wilfulness and independence and call them by the wrong name; what we call strength of will God looks upon as contemptible weakness. The Being with the greatest will who ever lived on the earth was Our Lord Jesus Christ, and yet He never exercised His will, as we think of will; His life was one of meekness and submission (*see* John v. 19, 30). Our Lord was the antipodes of the individual, there was nothing independent or wilful or self-assertive about Him, and He says 'Learn of Me, for I am meek and lowly in heart.' Jesus Christ cannot give me a meek and quiet spirit, I have to take His yoke upon me; that is, I have to deliberately discipline myself. The teaching of the Sermon on the Mount is the destruction of individuality and the exaltation of personality. When the personal life is merged with God, it will manifest the characteristics of God. Individuality never exhibits the characteristics of God but natural characteristics, the characteristics of Ishmael, or of Esau, or of Saul of Tarsus, that mock at the meek and lowly Son of God. What is it that begins to mock in you? 'Meek? Do you think I am going to bow my neck to that? Be loyal there, in my home? Obey a passing sentiment that came to me in a prayer meeting?' Cast out 'the bondwoman and her son'—the natural life and all that nourishes it, or it will lead your personal life to ruin. The casting out must be done by you, then God will bring it back into its rightful inheritance. The natural life can only be brought into union by being cast out (cf. Matt. vv. 29, 48).

If we do not resolutely cast out the natural, the supernatural can never become natural in us. There are some Christians in whom the supernatural and the natural seem one and the same, and you say—Well, they are not one with me, I find the natural at 'loggerheads' with the spiritual. The reason is that the other life has gone through the fanatical stage of cutting off the right arm, gone through the discipline of maiming the natural, completely casting it out, and God has brought it back into its right relationship with the spiritual on top, and the spiritual manifests itself in a life which knows no division into sacred and secular. There is no royal road there, each one has it entirely in his own hands; it is not a question of praying but of performing.

(III) THE OSTRACISM OF THE NATURAL. v. 14

The casting out of Hagar and Ishmael is necessary, but Hagar is not divorced. Divorce stands for apostasy (cf. Isaiah l: 1). We must be *divorced* from

104

sin, not separated from sin. Sin belongs to hell and
the devil; I, as a child of God, belong to heaven and
God, and I must have nothing to do with sin in any
shape or form. The separation which goes on all
through the life of faith is alluded to by Paul in Gal.
ii. 20—'I have been crucified with Christ'; and again
in Romans xii. 1—'Present your bodies a living sacrifice'—go to the funeral of your own independence.
It is not a question of giving up sin, but of giving
up my right to myself, my natural independence and
self-assertiveness. Immediately I do, the natural
cries out and goes through terrific suffering. There
are things in me which must go through death or they
will abide alone and ruin the personal life (cf. John xii.
24). But if I sternly put them through death, God
will bring them back into the right inheritance.
Jesus says 'If any man will be My disciple, let him
deny himself', i.e., deny his right to himself, and a
man has to realize Who Jesus Christ is before he will
do it. It is the things that are right and noble and
good from the natural standpoint that keep us back
from God's best. To discern that the natural virtues
antagonize surrender to God, is to begin to see where
the battle lies. It is going to cost the natural everything, not something.

(IV) THE ORDEAL OF THE NATURAL. v. 15—18

Beware of blaspheming the Creator by calling the
natural sinful. The natural is not sinful, but un-moral
and un-spiritual. It is the home of all the vagrant
vices and virtues, and must be disciplined with the
utmost severity until it learns its true position in the
providence of God. Remember, Abraham had to offer
up Ishmael before he offered up Isaac. Some of us
are trying to offer spiritual sacrifices before we have
sacrificed the natural. The only way we can offer a
spiritual sacrifice to God is to do what He tells us to
do, discipline what He tells us to discipline. Under

no consideration must we dictate to God on the basis of the natural life. When God's Son tells me to do a thing, I have no business to allow the natural to dictate and say—I cannot do that because I get so tired. What does it matter if it kills the natural? God's purpose for the natural will be fulfilled, I have to be absolutely stern with it and not make God wait on my natural inclinations.

(v) THE OUTRANCE OF THE NATURAL. v. 19—21

'Outrance'—the utmost extremity or bitter end. v. 20 is striking—'God was with the lad', as long as he remained in the straits of the desert, and he found his home in the oases and by the wells. After Ishmael had learned by experience that he was not a fellow heir with Isaac, he was richly endowed by Abraham, and he also remained in friendly relationship with Isaac (Ch. xxv. 9). God is not with my natural life as long as I pamper it and pander to it, but when I put it out in the desert, resolutely cast it out and keep it under, then God is with it and He opens up wells and oases, and fulfils His promise for it. It must be stern discipline, rigorous severity to the last degree on my part (cf. 1 Cor. ix. 27), then God will be with the natural life and bring it to its full purpose.

CONDITIONS

Genesis xxi. 22—34

'Now, who shall arbitrate?
　　Ten men love what I hate,
Shun what I follow, slight what I receive;
　　Ten, who in ears and eyes
　　Match me: we all surmise,
They this thing, and I that: whom shall my soul
　　believe?

'But I need, now as then,
　　Thee, God, who mouldest men;
And since, not even while the whirl was worst,
　　Did I,—to the wheel of life
　　With shapes and colours rife,
Bound dizzily,—mistake my end, to slake Thy thirst.'

Browning

'Thus they made a covenant at Beer-sheba.'　v. 32

The life of faith as portrayed in the life of Abraham
is a detailed presentation of its majesties and its
muddles.　We have detected Abraham's blunder in
the actual conditions in working from his wits, but
we must not forget that by far the most striking thing
about Abraham is his worship of God.

In this chapter the right relation between common
sense and faith is exhibited.　Common sense is not faith
and faith is not common sense; they stand in the
relation of Ishmael and Isaac, of the natural and the
spiritual, of individuality and personality, of impulse
and inspiration.　Faith in antagonism to common
sense is fanaticism, and common sense in antagonism
to faith is rationalism.　The life of faith brings
the two into right relationship.　No one can solve
the difficulty of making them one for me, I must

do it for myself, and I can only solve it by life not by thinking, just as the natural can only be made spiritual in life, not in thinking. We have the idea that the body, individuality, and the natural life are altogether of the devil; they are not, they are of God, designed by God, and it is in the human body and in the natural order of things that we have to exhibit our worship of God. The danger is to mistake the natural for the spiritual, and instead of worshipping God in my natural life to make my natural life God.

How am I going to find out what the will of God is? In one way only, by not trying to find out. If you are born again of the Spirit of God, you *are* the will of God, and your ordinary common-sense decisions are God's will for you unless He gives an inner check. When He does, call a halt immediately and wait on Him. Be renewed in the spirit of your mind that you may make out His will, not in your mind, but in practical living. God's will in my common-sense life is not for me to *accept* conditions and say—'Oh well, it is the will of God', but to *apprehend* them for Him, and that means conflict, and it is of God that we conflict. Doing the will of God is an active thing in my common-sense life.

(I) THE ARBITRATION BETWEEN ABRAHAM AND ABIMELECH. v. 22—24

Abimelech does not stand for the sinful, but for the noble and upright and perfectly natural. The blessing of God is recognized by the natural, but never recognized by the sinful. Abimelech stands as the type of civilization with its organizations and culture and good sense. Between the Church, which is an organism, and organization which is pagan, there must be arbitration. Much of our organization in the Church is pagan, and it is our salvation to see that it is pagan. Immediately we forget this and compromise instead of arbitrate, we have sold the Son of God to the world.

The attitude of faith to organization is illustrated in Our Lord's attitude to Pilate. Our Lord did not compromise with Pilate, He arbitrated with him—'You have to decide this matter because God has put you in the position where you must. You stand there on your dignity as proconsul: I stand here on My dignity as Son of God. If you put Me to death as your duty, I go to death because it is My duty.' There is no compromise there. 'If My kingdom *were* of this world, then would My servants fight' (John xviii. 36); but there is no fight, there is arbitration, and the reason for it is God's order behind the whole thing.

(II) THE APPREHENSION OF ABIMELECH BY ABRAHAM.
v. 25—26

Abraham distinguishes clearly between political and private rights in this matter of the well, and now he in his turn administers a rebuke to Abimelech. In v. 26 Abimelech throws back the reproof on Abraham on the plea that he had not been told that the well had been taken away. This of course is mere natural shrewdness, and is the ground of their first arbitration. It is instructive to notice that Abraham always takes his rebukes magnificently, he never once shows individuality but always personality.

When first we become spiritual we arbitrate with our bodies until we say—I will put the natural into absolute subjection and have no more arbitration (*see* 1 Cor. ix. 27). The same kind of thing is taking place in the history of the world to-day. At present there is arbitration between the children of God and the natural forces of civilization. We arbitrate between the two by recognizing the present claims of each without compromising either. When the Lord Jesus comes again there will be no more arbitration, all the natural forces of civilization will instantly be put in subjection to Him, in the same way that those who enter into the sanctified life deliberately put the natural in themselves into subjection to Jesus Christ. In the meantime there is arbitration, no compromise and no fight, but deliberate arbitration between the two.

As Abimelech rebuked Abraham when he was in the wrong (*see* Ch. xx), and Abraham in his turn rebuked Abimelech, so in the same way the children of men from time to time rebuke the children of God, and the children of God rebuke the politics of natural men. Compromise with each other or unity between them is immoral. Arbitration until He comes 'whose right it is to reign' is the God-ordained programme.

Abimelech exhibits the characteristic of natural, noble, worldly civilization which recognizes the blessing of God attached to the people of God, and shrewdly realizes the value of having the people of God in the midst of civilized life. No man on earth 'pooh-poohs' the people of God, although he himself does not intend to become one of them. Our Lord did not pray that His disciples should be taken out of the world, but that they should be kept from the evil (John xvii. 10).

(III) THE AGREEMENT OF ABRAHAM AND ABIMELECH.
v. 27—34

The Old Testament Scriptures always regard the oath as a peculiar sacrament. If you read what the Bible says about vowing you will see how culpably negligent we are in the way we promise. If we do not fulfil a promise, we damage our moral and spiritual life. It is infinitely better to refuse to promise anything, even in the most superficial relationships, than to promise and not perform. Spiritual leakages are accounted for in this way. Always do what you ought to do, but be careful of promising anything, because a promise puts the blood of God on your character.

If you make a promise you must see that it is fulfilled, no matter what it costs you. The glib way we promise is indicative of the slipshod ways we have got into, and of our laziness and indifference. The word of a natural man is his bond; the word of a saint binds God. It is a question of relationship to God all through.

The origin of the phrase 'business is business' is in the fact that business must not be carried on as a matter of faith but as a matter of covenant. Business is the go-between between the children of God and natural civilized life, and must be carried on by bonds.

By means of this arbitration Abraham's faith develops more fully into faith in the eternal truth of Jehovah's covenant (v. 33).

my child because I loved her too much.' Go through the crucible, and you will find that in it you learned to know God better.

(II) THE CONCENTRATION OF ABRAHAM.

'Behold, here I am.' v. 1.

These words express the greatest application of the human mind. To say 'Here I am' when God speaks, is only possible if we are in His presence, in the place where we can obey. To understand where I am in the sight of God means not only to listen but to obey promptly all He says. I can always know where I am. Whenever I want to debate about doing what I know to be supremely right, I am not in touch with God.

(III) THE COMMAND TO ABRAHAM.

'Take now thy son, thine only son Isaac, whom thou lovest . . .' v. 2.

God's words are, as it were, blows aimed against the incrustations of natural individual life in order that Abraham's personal faith might be emancipated into fellowship with God. The blows are aimed at individuality because individuality will not come into fellowship with God; personality always does. Individuality is the husk of the personality, the home of independence and pride; but when God is developing the faith of a man all that must be sacrificed. It is the chrysalis developing into a butterfly, a winged creature of personal life. If you are not in the crucible yourself, the blows seem cruel; but if you are, you find the ecstasy of being brought into personal fellowship with God. Faith always works on the personal line (cf. Job. i, 12).

God's command is—'Take *now* . . .,' not presently. To go to the height God shows can never be done presently, it must be done now. Every mother who gives her son in war-time climbs to the height instantly, there may be any amount of protest, but she climbs to the height and buries her son; her woman's heart goes through the bereavement long before it comes actually.

(IV) THE CLIMB FOR ABRAHAM.

'And offer him there for a burnt offering upon one of the mountains which I will tell thee of.' v. 2.

The mount of the Lord is the very height of the trial into which God brings His servant. There is no indication of the cost to Abraham, his implicit understanding of God so far out-reaches his explicit knowledge that he trusts God utterly and climbs the highest height on which God can ever prove him, and remains unutterably true to God. There was no conflict, that was over, Abraham's confidence was fixed; he did not consult with flesh and blood, his own or anyone else's, he instantly obeyed. The point is that though all other voices should proclaim differently, obedience to the dictates of the Spirit of God at all costs is to be the attitude of the faithful soul. This mountain is not a mountain of sacrifice, but the mountain of proof that Abraham loved God supremely (see v. 12).

It is extraordinary how we debate with right. We know a thing is right but we try to seek excuses for not doing it now. Always beware when you want to confer with your own flesh and blood, i.e., your own sympathies, your own insight. These things are based on individuality, not on personal relationship to God, and they are the things that compete with God and hinder our faith. When Our Lord is bringing us into personal relationship with Himself, it is always the individual relationships He breaks down. He comes with a sword rap on the husks that will not break, that will not let the life out for God. (Matt. x. 34.) 'If any man comes to Me and hate not . . ., he cannot be My disciple.' (Luke xiv. 26.) If you are outside the crucible you will say that Jesus Christ is cruel.

(I) THE DUTY OF DILIGENCE.

'And Abraham rose up early in the morning.' v. 3.

This phrase is characteristic not only of men and women in the Bible, but of God Himself. The revelation of God in the Old Testament is that of a working God. No other religion presents God either as diligent or as suffering, but as an all-in-all principle, ruling in lofty disdain. The God Who reveals Himself to Abraham is One ever intent on the fulfilment of His great designs; and like God, like people. If God is diligent, surely we ought to be diligent in doing our duty to Him. Think how patient and how diligent God has been with us! Over and over again God gets us near the point, and then by some petty individual sulk we spoil it all, and He patiently begins all over again. Think of the vision, 'whiter than snow shine', God gave of what He wanted us to be—where has it gone this Easter time? Has God had to begin all over again from where we left off last time, or have we said—I will be true to God at all costs, no matter what the isolation?

(II) THE DIRECTION OF DUTY.

'And went unto the place of which God had told him. v. 3.

Abraham took the direction of his duty from God's word, not from his own discernment (cf. Gen. xii. 4; Heb. xi. 8). Our danger is to water down God's word to suit ourselves. God never fits His word to suit me; He fits me to suit His word. The discernment of God's call does not come in every moment of life, but only in rare moments; the moments Our Lord spoke of as 'the light' (John xii. 35—36). We have to remain true to what we see in those moments; if we do not, we will put back God's purpose in our life. The undercurrent of regret arises when we confer with those who have not heard the call of God, and if we listen to them we get into darkness. The life of Abraham is an illustra-

118

tion of two things: of unreserved surrender to God, and of God's complete possession of a child of His for His own highest ends.

It is never the consecration of our gifts that fits us for God's service. Profoundly speaking, we are not here to work for God. Absorption in practical work is one of the greatest hindrances in preventing a soul discerning the call of God. Unless active work is balanced by a deep isolated solitude with God, knowledge of God does not grow and the worker becomes exhausted and spent out. Our Lord said that the only men He will use in His enterprises are those in whom He has done everything (Luke xiv. 26, 27, 33); otherwise we would serve our own ends all the time. Many have begun well but have gone off on doctrine, all their energy is spent furthering a cause, Jesus Christ is not the dominating ruler. The direction of duty lies not in doing things for God, but in doing what God tells us to do, and God's order comes to us in the haphazard moments. We do not make the haphazard moments, God is the arranger of the haphazard. The direction of duty is loyalty to God in our present circumstances.

(III) THE DISCIPLINE OF DISTANCE.
   'Then on the third day . . .' v. 4.

God is never in a hurry. We say, 'I see what God wants and it seems so easy, I wish I could do it now.' Abraham had to travel many long hours to the place of sacrifice, a deed was to be done after days of reflection, not on the impulse of the moment, and during the journey not a look or a word betrayed his secret. Isaac never guessed at the isolation in his father's mind. Never reveal to anyone the profound depths of your isolation; when the life is going on profoundly with God, conceal it. 'Appear not unto men to fast.' It was this about Our Lord that staggered the Pharisees, no one knew what He was going through in the profoundest concerns of His life. And at the end when He might easily have been absorbed in the tremendous issue which He knew was at hand, He revealed no concern about Himself, only for His disciples—'Let not your heart be troubled.'

(IV) THE DECEPTION OF DETERMINATION.

'I and the lad . . . will come again to you.' v. 5.

The strength of Abraham's faith appears in that he held to God's promise while he promptly went to do what seemed to prevent its fulfilment. He believed that God would fulfil all He had promised and did not stay to question. To take God at His word may mean expecting God to come up to my standard; whereas true faith does not so much take God at His word as take the word of God as it is, in the face of all difficulties, and act upon it, with no attempt to explain or expound it.

(V) THE DEVOTION OF THE DEVOTED.

'And Abraham took the wood of the burnt offering, and laid it upon Isaac his son.' v. 6.

This verse is sublime. There is nothing more wonderful than the picture of this thoughtful, obedient boy going with his father, and even when he knew what the purpose was (v. 9), he was willing to relinquish the joy of life (cf. John xxi. 18).

THE PATH OF GOD

Genesis xxii. 7—14

'My God, my God, let me for once look on thee
As though nought else existed, we alone!
And as creation crumbles, my soul's spark
Expands till I can say,—Even from myself
I need thee and I feel thee and I love thee.
I do not plead my rapture in thy works
For love of thee, nor that I feel as one
Who cannot die: but there is that in me
Which turns to thee, which loves or which should
    love.'   *Browning*

'God will provide Himself . . .' v. 8.

The life of Abraham provides the pattern spiritual
biography in which the life ascends from the rational
and accountable to the personally traced footsteps
of the soul's path to God. The turning points in the
spiral ascent of faith are, first, obedience to the
effectual call of God (ch. xii); and second, the culmin-
ation of unreserved resignation to God (ch. xxii).
Our difficulties spiritually arise from unrecognized
spiritual hysterics, in which mood we unconsciously
select God to watch us and our symptoms. The only
cure for that is to get hold of God and have no
symptoms.

(I) THE SPEECH OF SILENT SPIRITUALITY. v. 7—8

The speech of Abraham and Isaac reveals that they
are spiritually silent—the son is silent before the father
as the father is silent before God, and thus God
elevates them both above unspiritual human nature.
That is, both father and son have gone one step beyond
the limit of the possible because they are on the path

of God. To talk easily about spiritual experiences is an indication that I have only a devout nodding acquaintance with the experiences of others, and am devoid of all such experiences myself.

In the life of faith the pressure of forethought is transferred to God by the faith which fulfils His behests; I have faith in God's accountable rationality, not in my own. If I have never heard the call of God, all I see is the accountability that I can state to myself. Practical work is nearly always a determination to think for myself, to take the pressure of forethought on myself: I see the need, therefore I must do something. That is not the effectual call of God, but the call of my sympathy with conditions as I see them. When God's call comes, I learn to do actively what He tells me and take no thought for the morrow. Take a step in faith in God, and your rational friends will say: 'Very beautiful, but suppose we all did it . . .!' You are not living on the line of accountable rationality, but a life of agreement with God's effectual call, and have therefore no reply to make.

In Hebrews xi. 19 we get an insight into Abraham's spirituality—'Accounting that God was able to raise him up, even from the dead.' It was not Abraham's common sense but his spiritual illumination that made him know it. Beware of turning a common-sense somersault and make God appear foolish by saying that Abraham knew all about it and it was not a sacrifice at all. Abraham did not know all about it; he believed that God would give Isaac back to him, but how, he had no notion; he surrendered himself entirely to the supernatural God. God never tells us what He is going to do, He reveals Who He is.

'So they went both of them together' in the obedience of faith. Abraham stood in the midst of the most appalling personal controversy, the controversy between natural love and faith, and Isaac was worthy

122

of his father. The path *to* God is never the same as the path *of* God. When I am going on with God in His path, I do not understand, but God does; therefore I understand God, not His path. When you take a step in faith in God and fulfil His behests, God does the forethinking for you. When you do it for yourself, God has to take second place. If you are going through the discipline of transferring your forethought to God and actively fulfilling His behests, you have to be silent; and when you do speak your speech is shallow, it does not convey where you are. People must never guess what you are going through. Piety always pretends to be going through what it is not.

(II) THE SACRIFICE OF SURRENDERED SONSHIP. v. 9—10

God is the ruling factor in all our transactions (cf. Proverbs xx. 24). When we commit ourselves to God He arranges the haphazard, and we have to see that we actively fulfil His behests where He places us.

The binding of Isaac is a prefiguring of the fulfilment and the perfection of the Death of Christ. The emphasis of the so-called Higher Christian Life is to look at Christ as our Example, not as our sacrifice: by prayer and consecration we come into God's favour. We do not, that is blasphemy. God never accepts us because we obey; He can only accept us on the ground of sacrifice, which cost death. Therefore our approach to God can never be on the ground of our merit— that I am being bound by Another; that is the effect of the sacrifice of Christ in me. Personal holiness is never the ground of my acceptance with God; the only ground of acceptance is the Death of the Lord Jesus Christ.

(III) THE SYMPATHY OF SUPREME SPIRIT. v. 11—12

Abraham had a rational understanding of what God's command meant and he had to step out of it. Abraham was not a fanatic, the instant the voice of

God came he surrendered himself in devotion to the voice, although it seemed an arrest of obedience to the Divine command. The essence of true religious faith is devotion to a Person. Beware of sticking to convictions instead of to Christ; convictions are simply the clothes of your growing life.

The great point of Abraham's faith in God was that he was prepared to do anything for God. Mark the difference between that and doing anything to *prove* your love to God. Abraham was there to obey God, no matter to what he went contrary. Abraham was not a pledged devotee of his own convictions, or he would have slain his son and said the voice of the angel was the voice of the devil. There is always the point of giving up convictions and traditional beliefs. If I will remain true to God, He will lead me straight through the ordeal into the inner chamber of a better knowledge of God. Our Lord taught us to pray 'lead us not into temptation.' Don't ask God to test you. Don't declare as Peter did, I will do anything, I will go to death for You. Abraham did not make any such declaration, he remained true to God, and God purified his faith.

Abraham is taught by the ancient ritual what Paul clearly expressed in Romans xii. 1. v. 9 is a picture of the blunder of thinking that the sacrifice of death is the final thing God wants: what God wants is the sacrifice through death which enables a man to do what Jesus did, viz. sacrifice his life. Many of us think that God wants us to give up things; we make Christianity the great apotheosis of giving up! God purified Abraham from this blunder, and the same discipline goes on in our lives. 'Oh well, I expect God will ask me to give that up.' God nowhere tells us to give up things for the sake of giving them up; He tells us to give them up for the sake of the only thing worth having, viz. life with Himself. It is a question of loosening the bands that hinder our life,

and immediately those bands are loosened by identification with the death of Jesus, we enter into a
relationship with God whereby we sacrifice our life
to God. To give God my life for death is of no value;
what is of value is to let Him have all my powers that
have been saved and sanctified, so that as Jesus
sacrificed His life for His Father, I can sacrifice my
life for Him. 'Present your bodies a *living* sacrifice,'
says Paul.

(IV) THE SUBSTITUTION OF SACRAMENTAL SERVICE.
v. 13—14

Abraham did not receive a positive command to
sacrifice the ram, he recognized in the ram caught by
his horns in a thicket behind him a Divine suggestion.
Until we get into fellowship with God His suggestions
are no good to us. When people are intimate with one
another suggestions convey more than words, and
when God gets us into oneness with Himself we recognize His suggestions. Abraham offers the ram as a
substitute for his son; he does not withhold his son
in intention, although in fact he offers a substitute.
The entire system of sacrifice is an extension of the
sacrifice of the ram. The spiritual sacrifice of Isaac
and the physical sacrifice of the ram are made one,
the natural and the spiritual are blended. That
Christ is the substitute for me and therefore I go
scot free, is never taught in the New Testament. If
I say that Christ suffered instead of me, I knock the
bottom board out of His sacrifice. *Christ died in the
stead of me.* I, a guilty sinner, can never get right with
God, it is impossible. I can only be brought into union
with God by identification with the One Who died
in my stead. No sinner can get right with God on any
other ground than the ground that Christ died *in his
stead*, not *instead of him*.

THE ETERNAL GOAL

Genesis xxii. 15—19

'My goal is God Himself, not joy, nor peace,
　Nor even blessing, but Himself, my God;
'Tis His to lead me there, not mine, but His—
　"At any cost, dear Lord, by any road!"

One thing I know, I cannot say Him nay;
　One thing I do, I press towards my Lord;
My God my glory here, from day to day,
　And in the glory there my Great Reward.'
F. Brook

'In blessing I will bless thee . . . because thou hast
obeyed My voice.' v. 17—18

The spirit of obedience gives more joy to God than
anything else on earth. Obedience is impossible to us
naturally, even when we do obey, we do it with a pout
in our moral underlip, and with the determination
to scale up high enough and then 'boss my boss'. In
the spiritual domain there is no pout to be removed
because the nature of God has come into me. The
nature of God is exhibited in the life of Our Lord,
and the great characteristic of His life is obedience.
When the love of God is shed abroad in my heart by
the Holy Ghost (Romans v. 5), I am possessed by the
nature of God, and I show by my obedience that I
love Him. The best measure of a spiritual life is not
its ecstasies, but its obedience. 'To obey is better
than sacrifice.'

(I) THE SUPREME CALL OF GOD. v. 15
　When God first called to Abraham there was still a
dim gulf between them, God had to call and Abraham

126

to answer (v. 1). Now that gulf is bridged. 'The angel of the Lord called a second time out of heaven . . .,' i.e., an inward state of soul, and Abraham is so near to God that he does not need to reply; he is in the place of unimpeded listening. Is there any impediment between my ears and God's voice?

The call of God is a call in accordance with the nature of God, not in accordance with my idea of God. At first, Abraham did not interpret the call along the line of the nature of God because he did not know it; he interpreted it along the line of the Chaldaic tradition and took it to mean he was to kill his son. The supreme crisis in Abraham's faith has now been reached, all his imperfect conceptions of God have been left behind and he has come now to understand God. Always beware of self-assertiveness, it bruises our relationship to God, and distorts the manifestation of His nature in us. Abraham was neither an amateur providence nor a moral policeman, he simply believed God.

(II) THE SUPREME REALITY OF GOD. v. 16

Abraham has come to the place where he is in touch with the very nature of God, he understands the reality of God, and God, as it were, unveils Himself to him in a burst of enthusiasm. There is no possibility of questioning on my part when God speaks, if He is speaking to His own nature in me; prompt obedience is the only result. When Jesus says 'Come unto Me,' I simply come; when He says 'Trust in God in this matter,' I do not try to trust, I *do* trust. An alteration has taken place in my disposition which is an evidence that the nature of God is at work in me.

(III) THE SUPREME CHARACTER OF GOD. v. 17—18

The promise of God stands in relation to Abraham's tried and willing obedience. The revelation of God

to me is determined by my character, not by God's
(Psalm xviii. 25—26). If I am mean, that is how God
will appear to me.

> 'Tis because I am mean, Thy ways so oft
> Look mean to me.'

By the discipline of obedience, I come to the
place Abraham reached and see God as He is.
The promises of God are of no use to me until by
obedience I understand the nature of God. We
read some things in the Bible three hundred and
sixty-five times and they mean nothing to us, then
all of a sudden we see what they mean, because in
some particular we have obeyed God, and instantly
His character is revealed. 'For how many soever be
the promises of God, in Him is the yea.' The 'yea'
must be born of obedience; when by the obedience of
our life, we say 'Amen', 'So let it be', to a promise,
then that promise is made ours.

(IV) THE SUPREME REWARD. v. 19

The more we have to sacrifice for God, the more
glorious is the reward presently. We have no right to
choose our sacrifice, God will let us see where the
sacrifice is to come, and it will always be on the
line of what God has given us, our 'Isaac', and yet
His call is to sacrifice it. God is always at work on the
principle of lifting up the natural and making it and
the spiritual one, and very few of us will go through
with it. We will cling to the natural when God wants
to put a sword through it. If you go through the
transfiguration of the natural, you will receive it back
on a new plane altogether. God wants to make
eternally our own what we only possessed inter-
mittently.

In the beginning we do not train for God, we train
for work, for our own aims, but as we go on with God
we lose all our own aims and are trained into God's

128

purpose. Unless practical work is appointed by God, it will prove a curse (cf. John xvii. 18). 'At any cost, by any road,' means nothing self-chosen. The Bible does not say that God blessed Abraham and took him to heaven; but that He blessed him and kept him on earth. The maturity of character before God is the personal channel through which He can bless others. If it takes all our lifetime before God can put us right, then others are going to be impoverished. We need to hurry and climb our Mount Moriah, come to the place where God can put an end to the dim gulf between Him and ourselves, then He will be able to bless us as He did Abraham.

No language can express the ineffable blessedness of the supreme reward that awaits the soul that has taken its supreme climb, proved its supreme love, and entered on its supreme reward. What an imperturbable certainty there is about the man who is in contact with the real God! Thank God, the life of the Father of the Faithful is but a specimen of the life of every humble believer who obediently follows the dicipline of the life of faith. What a depth of transparent rightness there must be about the man who walks before God, and the meaning of the Atonement is to place us there in perfect adjustment to God. 'Walk before Me, and be thou perfect,' not faultless, but blameless, undeserving of censure in the eyes of God.

STILL HUMAN

Genesis xxii. 20—24

'For some may follow truth from dawn to dark
As a child follows by his mother's hand,
Knowing no fear, rejoicing all the way;
And unto some her face is as a star
Set through an avenue of thorns and fires,
And waving branches, black without a leaf.

And still it draws them, though the feet must bleed,
Though the garments must be rent and eyes be
  scorched;
And if the valley of the shadow of death
Be passed, and to the level road they come,
Still with their faces to the polar star,
It is not with the same looks, the same limbs,
But halt and maimed and of infirmity.'

'And it came to pass . . . that it was told Abraham.'
v. 20.

(I) GOD'S OMNISCIENCE AND HUMAN LIFE.

What the natural reason would call an anti-climax
is the very climax of God's supernatural grace whereby
a man having gone through the most wonderful
experience, emerges and lives an unwonderful,
ordinary life. That is the difference between the
fanatic and the faithful soul. You find it all through
the New Testament. The wonder of the Incarnation
slips into the life of ordinary childhood; the marvel
of the Transfiguration descends to the valley and the
demon-possessed boy, and the glory of the Resurrec-
tion merges into Our Lord providing breakfast for
His disciples on the sea shore in the early dawn. The
tendency in early Christian experience is to look
for the marvellous. We are apt to mistake the sense
of the heroic for being heroes. It is one thing to go
through a crisis grandly, but a different thing to go

through every day glorifying God when there is no witness, no limelight, and no one paying the remotest attention to you. If we don't want medieval haloes, we want something that will make people say— What a wonderful man of prayer he is! What a pious, devoted woman she is! If anyone says that of you, you have not been loyal to God. If you are rightly devoted to Jesus Christ, you have reached the sublime height where no one thinks of noticing you, all that is noticed is that the power of God comes through all the time. It is along some such line as this that we are to understand the omniscience of God and human life. 'Oh, I have had a wonderful call from God!' It takes Almighty God Incarnate in you to peel potatoes properly, and to wash heathen children for the glory of God. *Anyone* cannot do these things; anybody can do the shining in the sun and the sporting in the footlights, but it takes God's incarnated Spirit to make you so absolutely humanly His that you are utterly unnoticeable.

(II) GOD'S OBJECT AND HUMAN NATURE.

The history of the life of Abraham does not close abruptly with his greatest act of faith, but from that act of faith there is a natural human progress to a sanctified life. Human nature likes to read about the heroic and the intense: it takes the Divine nature to be interested in grass and sparrows and trees, because they are so unutterably commonplace, and also because God happens to have made them. God's order is the human; the devil's is the spectacular. The object of the crisis is that we may live the human life in perfect relation to God.

Abraham is not the type of a saint or of sanctification, but of the life of faith. Our human relationships are the actual conditions in which the ideal life of God is to be exhibited. Any sordid being can sit in a cathedral in the twilight and listen to beautiful music

131

and feel divine; Abraham lived as God's man in the earthly conditions of his life. If the indwelling of God cannot be manifested in human flesh, then the Incarnation and the Atonement are of no avail. All our Christian work may be merely scaffolding poles to prepare us so that God may do what He likes with us, unobtrusively. The test of the life of a saint is not success, but faithfulness as a steward of the mysteries of God in human life as it actually is (cf. Luke vi. 40). We will put up success as the aim in Christian work; the one thing glorifying to God is the glory of God manifested in human lives unobtrusively. The 'show business' belongs to the pagan order of things; devotion to God in actual human conditions belongs to the Redemptive order. A Christian is one who has learned to live the life hid with Christ in God in human conditions.

(III) GOD'S ORDER AND HUMAN HAPHAZARD. v. 20

The message which Abraham received was providential and came at the right moment. The message was apparently haphazard, but it was all in the order of God. It is a great moment in the life of a child of God when letters and messages are seen to be under the direction of Divine providence. When God brings me a word on occasions and I obey it, He will look after everything else. There is nothing haphazard to a child of God (Romans viii. 28).

(IV) GOD'S OPPORTUNITY AND HUMAN FORETHOUGHT. v. 21-23

Abraham must soon think of Isaac's marriage, and the message from his kindred causes him to hope that he may find in his brother's family a bride for Isaac. Remain true to God in your obscurity, and remember you are not the designer of your destiny. You hear the call of God and realize what He wants, then you begin to find reasons why you should not obey Him. Well, obey Him, because away in some other part of the world there are other circumstances being worked by God, and if you say—'I shan't, I wasn't made for this,' you get out of touch with God. Your 'goings' are not according to your mind, but according to God's mind. Remain true at all costs to what God is doing with you and don't ask why He is doing it. Don't loaf along like a strayed poet on the fringes of God's providence; the Almighty has got you in hand, leave yourself alone and trust in Him. Half the sentimental pious folks that strew the coasts of emotional religious life are there because we will engineer our own circumstances. We have to be for God's purpose, and God cannot explain His purpose until it happens. God's omniscience, God's order, and God's opportunity in my individual life all work together, and Jesus Christ enters into my life just at the point of the haphazard circumstances I am in. Sanctification is not the end of Redemption, it is the gateway to the purpose of God. No Christian experience is the end and purpose of Redemption. God's own plans are the purpose of Redemption.

When the call of Jesus Christ comes, it comes to *you*, it cannot come to your father or your mother, or to your wife, or to your own self-interest; it comes entirely to your personal life. Instantly the clamour begins. Father and mother say No, the claims of my own life say No; Jesus Christ says Yes. Think—could Jesus Christ's call mean that I hurt my father and mother irrevocably? Certainly it could not; then if I obey Him, even though it looks like bringing the sword and the upset into lives, in the final wind up God will bring His wisdom out perfectly, and I shall find that every one of those human relationships have been brought in in the wake of my obedience. The point is—will I trust God, or lean to my own convictions? Obedience to the supremacy of the Lord Jesus is the only legitimate outcome of sanctification. Thank God, He wants us to be human, not spooks!

HUMAN GREATNESS

Genesis xxiii

'We cannot kindle when we will
　　The fire which in the heart resides;
The spirit bloweth and is still,
　　In mystery our soul abides.
　　　　But tasks in hours of insight will'd
　　　　Can be through hours of gloom fulfill'd.

With aching hands and bleeding feet,
　　We dig and heap, lay stone on stone;
We bear the burden and the heat
　　Of the long day, and wish 'twere done.
　　　　Not till the hours of light return
　　　　All we have built do we discern.'

Matthew Arnold

'Thou art a prince of God.'　v. 6

(I) IN THE PLACE OF SORROW. v. 1—2

The Old Testament relates the end of no other woman's life so particularly as it does the end of Sarah's life. Abraham's personal sorrow is recorded in the words—'to weep for her.' It is a farce to make nothing of death; the natural expressions of the heart are not suppressed, but tempered and transfigured. It is no part of faith to affect insensibility to sorrow, that is stoical humbug. In certain stages of religious experience we have the idea that we must not show sorrow when we are sorrowful. That idea is an enemy to the Spirit of Jesus Christ, because it leads to heartlessness and hypocrisy. Not to sorrow is not even human, it is diabolical. The Spirit of God hallows sorrow.

In dealing with the life of Abraham as the Father

of the Faithful neither faith nor common sense must
be our guide, but God Who unites both in the alchemy
of personal experience. To be guided by common
sense alone is fanatical; both common sense and faith
have to be brought into relation to God. The life of
faith does not consist of acts of worship or of great
self-denial and heroic virtues, but of all the daily
conscious acts of our lives.

(II) IN THE PLACE OF SOJOURNING.   v. 3—4

The phrase Abraham uses, 'a stranger and sojourner,' is the inner meaning of the term 'Hebrew.'
Abraham could never say that he was at home in
Canaan, he left his home never to find another on
earth. The thought of pilgrimage sank deep into the
Hebrew mind, and the note of the sojourner is essen-
tially the note of the Christian. Instead of being
pilgrims and strangers on the earth, we become
citizens of this order of things and entrench ourselves
here, and the statements of Jesus have no meaning.
The genius of the Spirit of God is to make us pilgrims,
consequently there is the continual un-at-home-ness
in this world. (cf. Phil. iii. 20.) It is a matter of
indifference to the Spirit of God where we are, and it
ought to be equally indifferent to us. As saints, we
are cursed, not blessed, by patriotism. The idea of
nations is man's, not God's. When Our Lord establishes
His Kingdom there will be no nations, only the
great Kingdom of God. That is why His Kingdom is
not built up on civilized life.

(III) IN THE PLACE OF SENTIMENT.   v. 8—9

Sentiment is thought occasioned by feeling;
sentimentality is feeling occasioned by thought.
Sentiment plays an important part in human affairs,
and no sentiment is more sacred than that connected
with our dead. Sentimentality is produced by watch-
ing things we are not in. Go through a disaster or

bereavement, and the emotions produced are the bedrock of feeling which makes human life worthy. As Christians we should conduct our lives on the high sentiment which is the outcome of a transaction with the Lord Jesus Christ. If our testimony is hard, it is because we have gone through no crisis with God, there is no heartbroken emotion behind it. If we have been through a crisis in which human feeling has been ploughed to its inner centre by the Lord, our testimony will convey all the weight of the greatness of God along with human greatness. It is essential to go through a crisis with God which costs you something, otherwise your devotional life is not worth anything. You cannot be profoundly moved by nothing, or by doctrine; you can only be profoundly moved by devotion.

v. 8—9. The story of Abraham's palaver with the Hittites conveys the idea that they had respect for the true greatness of Abraham.

'Bending before men is a recognition that there does dwell in that presence of our brother something divine.'   *Carlyle*

We all recognize human trappings; only one in a thousand recognizes human greatness. We bow not to greatness, but to the trappings of money and of birth. If I bow because I must, I am a conventional fraud; if I bow because I recognize true greatness, it is a sign that I am being emancipated. The greatest humiliation for a Christian is to recognize that he has ignored true greatness because it was without trappings. If the Pharisees had been reverent towards true greatness, they would not have treated the Nazarene Carpenter as they did.

(IV) IN THE PLACE OF SCRUPULOSITY. v. 17—18

The details of this palaver must not be passed over. We are apt to say that religion is religion, and business

is business; but there is no cleavage in the life of
faith. Slovenliness is an insult to the Holy Ghost.
Our Lord is scrupulous in His saving of us, surely we
can be scrupulous in the conduct of His temple, our
bodies and our bodily connections. That will mean
God's greatness coming down into our human setting,
and we see to it that we do everything in keeping with
the greatness of God.

(v) IN THE PLACE OF SUBLIMITY. v. 6
The Hittites had no word for 'gentleman', so
they called Abraham 'a prince of God'. Abraham
kept company with God until he became a partaker
of the Divine nature. It is impossible for a saint, no
matter what his experience, to keep right with God
if he will not take the trouble to spend time with
God. In order to keep the mind and heart awake to
God's high ideals you have to keep coming back
again and again to the primal source. If you do not,
you will be crushed into degeneracy. Just as a poet
or an artist must keep his soul brooding on the right
lines, so a Christian must keep the sense of God's call
always awake. Spend plenty of time with God; let
other things go, but don't neglect Him. And beware
of practical work. We are not here to do work *for*
God, we are here to be workers *with* Him, those
through whom He can do His work.

BEATIFIC BETROTHAL

Genesis xxiv

'Warp and Woof and Tangle,—
    Weavers of Webs are we.
Living and dying—and mightier dead,
For the shuttle, once sped, is sped—is sped;—
    Weavers of Webs are we.

White, and Black, and Hodden-gray,—
    Weavers of Webs are we.
To every weaver one golden strand
Is given in trust by the Master-Hand;—
    Weavers of Webs are we.

And that we weave, we know not,—
    Weavers of Webs are we.
The threads we see, but the pattern is known
To the Master-Weaver alone, alone;—
    Weavers of Webs are we.

                                        John Oxenham

'Come in, thou blessed of the Lord; wherefore
standest thou without?' v. 31.

Nothing can exceed the dignity and beauty of this
chapter in the Bible. It reveals God's providential
workings in the lives of several elemental, upright
people, and clearly conveys God's order for each
one. In the case of Abraham we see sublime sentiment (thought born in profound feeling) being worked
out in plain common-sense details, yet with the
natural sensibilities alive at once to human conditions
and to the demands of God.

(I) SENTIMENT, SENSE AND SENSIBILITY.

As already stated, there is a difference between
sentiment and sentimentality. We cannot be profoundly moved by thought; we can only be pro-

foundly moved by a personal crisis with God in which our usual equilibrium is disturbed, and our subsequent conceptions of life must be taken from the emotions stirred by the crisis. If the disturbance comes to you from outside, you will be exactly the same after it; but if you go through a personal crisis, such as Our Lord insists on, the personal crisis of devotion to Himself in discipleship, then all your conceptions of life will take colour from that moment. People are called backsliders who are merely sentimental pious people, they have had no crisis, all they have is the affectation of sentimentality. Recall the depths of feeling through which God has taken Abraham, and now in this chapter we see him being led rightly in the actual concerns of life. Right views on profound subjects will always be the spring of right relationships in shallow matters. To be guided by common sense is as foolish as being guided by faith. God is the One Who welds both faith and common sense into one practical personality.

By 'Sense' understand matters of practical human existence, and remember that any feature of actual life not brought under the severe control of the conception born of your crisis with God will leave a loophole for the devil. For instance, if you ignore certain aspects of your natural life as it has been constructed by God—take too much sleep, or not enough sleep, forego meals—you will give occasion to the enemy straightaway, no matter how great a saint you are. We have no business to leave out any part of our being from the control of the conceptions born of our crisis with God. The difficulty with us as Christians is that we will not think in accordance with the crisis we have had; consequently when we come to the things of sense and meet with people who have not had a crisis with God, it is an easy business to climb down. If we remain true to the sentiment produced in us by our crisis with God, those who meantime protest against us will ultimately come up to the same standard; but if we succumb, everything will go down.

By 'Sensibility' understand the natural intuitive power usually called tact, which makes it possible for us to live with other people without annoying them. These three, sentiment, sense and sensibility, must be welded into one in our personal lives by devotion to the Lord Jesus Christ.

(II) SOLEMN SACREDNESS OF SERVING.

Eliezer in many respects stands as a picture of a disciple of the Lord; the whole moulding of his life is his devotion to another, not to a sense of right or duty, but to his master (cf. John xiii. 13—14). We know very little about devotion to Jesus Christ. We know about devotion to right and to duty, but none of that is saintly, it is purely natural. My sense of duty and of right can never be God's. If I can state what my duty is, I have become my god in that particular. There is only One Who knows what my duty is as a Christian, and that is God. The Sermon on the Mount nowhere tells us what our duty is; it tells us the things a saint will do—things that are not his duty, e.g., Matt. v. 39—42. Be renewed in the spirit of your mind, says Paul, not that you may do your duty, but that you may make out what God's will is.

All the reward Eliezer seeks is the happiness of his master, self-remembrance in him is dead. He is shrewd and practical, yet as guileless as a child, the exact embodiment of 1 Cor. iv. 2—'It is required in stewards, that a man be found *faithful*.'

(III) SELF-FORGETFULNESS IN STEWARDS OF SECRETS.

One significant thing to notice is that Rebecca came alone and unveiled, and conversed freely with a stranger. The self-forgetfulness of Eliezer and Rebecca's own intuition made her know that she was safe with him. 'Man's virtue and woman's liberty go hand in hand.' There are those who talk like angels, yet they smudge the soul; there are others who may not talk sweetly yet they exhilarate the soul. Guard your intuition as the gift of God. You cannot judge virtue by its obverse; you can only judge virtue by intuition. Woe be to any woman who ignores her intuition, ignores the warning which says —Now draw back. For God's sake and your own womanhood's sake, draw back, it matters not who the person is.

(IV) SWEET SUPREMACY OF SINGLENESS.

Rebecca's brother and mother recognize God's hand in the whole matter (v. 50), and Rebecca's consent is sought only on the point of departure. 'And she said, I will go.' Those words are the answer to Eliezer's prayer. Rebecca felt the thrill which always passes through any pure young heart in the presence of a saint. A soul's trust in a saint in the providence of God is something more precious even than love. Few of us know anything about it because we are too sordidly selfish, we want things for ourselves all the time. Eliezer had only one conception, loyalty to his master, and in the providence of God he brought Rebecca straight to Isaac. This marriage, like all true marriages, concerns the Kingdom of God.

DISCOVERING DIVINE DESIGNS

Genesis xxiv

'Let us not always say
   "Spite of this flesh to-day
I strove, made head, gained ground upon the whole!"
   As the bird wings and sings,
   Let us cry "All good things
Are ours, nor soul helps flesh more, now, than flesh
   helps soul!"

   He fixed thee mid this dance
   Of plastic circumstance,
This Present, thou, forsooth, wouldst fain arrest:
   Machinery just meant
   To give thy soul its bent,
Try thee and turn thee forth, sufficiently impressed.'
                              Browning

'And the man bowed down his head and worshipped
the Lord.' v. 26

The whole discipline of the life of faith is to make
the ideal visions of faith and the actual performance
of life one in personal possession. Only one Being
can enable us to make the ideal and the actual one in
personal life, viz., the Holy Spirit. In art and literature
the ideal and the actual are only made one in a picture
or a poem or book. The temple of the Holy Ghost is
our personal life.

(I) HUMAN FORETHOUGHT AND DIVINE DESIGN. v. 1—9
   Abraham's motive is clearly stated here. Never
speak of human motives as if they were opposed to
the Divine. In the life of a child of God the human
motive is the disguised Divine. Sanctification means
that I become a child of God, consequently my

common-sense decisions are God's will unless He gives the check of His Spirit. I decide things in perfect fellowship with God, knowing that if my decisions are wrong, He will check. When He checks, I must stop at once. It is the inner check of the Spirit that prevents common sense being our god. There are times of crisis when we must wait on God, but they are rare. It is the abortion of piety to ask God to guide us here and there, of course He will! Such asking is not real. Remember our Lord's injunction—'Except ye become as little children.'

If God is not recognized by His blessings in the details of actual life in the beginning, He will be recognized in the end by His destructions. Human forethought in a faithful soul such as Abraham is the manifestation of the Divine design. In looking back you see not the haphazard, but an amazing design which, if you are born of God, you will credit to God; otherwise you credit it to the extraordinary wisdom of men and women.

(II) HUMAN APPOINTMENTS AND DIVINE DISCOVERIES. v. 10—21

It is our wisdom to follow providence, but folly to force it. By earnest human effort Eliezer makes his appointments, and these are not only recognized by God, but become also discoveries of the Divine mind. Unless you are a saint, your praying is pious humbug; but if you are a saint, you soon realize that you discover the Divine by energetically doing the human, provided you are maintaining a personal relationship to God. The fanatical element in the saint is the element that is devoted to a principle instead of to consistent conduct before God. For instance, I may become a devotee to the doctrine of Divine healing which means I must never be sick, and if I am sick then I say I must have gone wrong. The battle all through is against the absurdity of being consistent to an ideal instead of to God. The vital point about Eliezer is not his asking for signs, but that *Eliezer* asked for signs. Eliezer was a man who related everything entirely to God, consequently his human appointments, which are easy to ridicule, were God's way of enabling him to discover His mind. Beware of making a fetish of consistency to convictions instead of developing your faith in God. 'I shall never do that' —in all probability you will have to if you are a saint. Whenever we take what God has done and put it in the place of Himself, we instantly become idolaters. If Our Lord had been fanatically consistent, He would have said after the temptation—I have not eaten for forty days, therefore I will never eat food again. He did not eat for forty days because it was His Father's will for Him not to. Judged on the line of logical consistency there was no more inconsistent being than Our Lord. He said—'Resist not evil'; and then He cleansed the temple in Jerusalem. (Mark xi. 15—16). But Our Lord was never inconsistent to His Father. The saint is to be consistent to the Divine life within him, not logically consistent to a principle. A fanatic is concerned not about God but about proving his own little fanatical ideas. It is a danger peculiar to us all. It is easier to be a fanatic than a faithful soul, because there is something amazingly humbling, particularly to our religious conceit, in being loyal to God.

(III) HUMAN ASTONISHMENT AND DIVINE DETAILS.
    v. 22—33

The details of these verses are commonplace to Eastern custom, but Eliezer sees God in them. It is easy to see God in exceptional things or in a crisis, but it requires the culture of spiritual discipline to see God in every detail. Never allow that the haphazard is anything less than God's appointed order.

One other thing to note in these verses is the

characteristic of the hospitality, it is an incurious, generous hospitality, which is the rarest type. Hospitality is characteristic not only of the East but of God's programme. To be curious about another person's affairs is an impertinence and is never Christian.

(IV) HUMAN AFFINITIES AND DIVINE DIRECTIONS
   v. 34—49
Eliezer gives a simple account of his journey, but his speech is an example of great wisdom. When the Spirit of God guides a man's human affairs, his speech indicates not human shrewdness, but the frankness of Divine skill. Ever note that we must be ready to discover the Divine designs *anywhere*.

(V) HUMAN ABANDON AND DIVINE DEVOTION. v. 50—67
The custom according to which the brother must interest himself in the affairs of the sister is the explanation of much in these verses. They recognized the will of God in the whole matter, and have neither good nor ill to say. The consent of Rebecca is not sought in the betrothal, but only in the less important point of immediate departure.

When a soul abandons to God, God will not abandon it. But let that soul trust its wits and become its own amateur providence and a dexterous muddle will be the result. When once you have the amateur providence idea, it will prevent your doing the thing God tells you to do—'I must not tell my parents about my call; I want to prevent them suffering.' Your plain duty before God is to tell them. If you are abandoned to God and do the duty that lies nearest, God will not abandon you; but if you trust in your wits and bring in the amateur providence idea, He will have to abandon you, and there will be heartbreaks and distresses that He is not in at all. Present the whole thing where it ought to be presented—in abandonment to God, and He will engineer everything in His own way.

145

SUNSET

Genesis xxv. 1—10

'That low man seeks a little thing to do,
  Sees it and does it:
This high man, with a great thing to pursue,
  Dies ere he know it.
That low man goes on adding one to one,
  His hundred's soon hit:
This high man, aiming at a million,
  Misses an unit.
That, has the world here—should he need the next,
  Let the world mind him!
This, throws himself on God, and unperplexed,
  Seeking shall find him.'

Browning

'And his sons Isaac and Ishmael buried him.' v. 9.

It is not what a man achieves, but what he believes and strives for that makes him noble and great. Hebrews xi impresses this aspect of the life of faith over against the life of human perfection. The first thing faith in God does is to remove all thought of relevant perfection. Some lives may seem humanly perfect and yet not be relevant to God and His purpose. The effect such lives leave is not of a reach that exceeds its grasp, but of a completed little circle of their own. It takes a man completely severed from God to be perfect in that way. There is a difference between a perfect human life lived on earth and a personal life with God lived on earth; the former grasps that for which it reaches, the latter is grasped by that which it never can reach. The former chains us to earth by its very completeness; the latter causes us to fling ourselves unperplexed on God. The differ-

146

ence is not a question of sin, but the paradox of the incomplete perfection of a right relationship to God.

(I) THE REGION OF THE IRRELEVANT. v. 1—4

One of the most striking features in Abraham's life is its irrelevancy. If we take Abraham to be the embodiment of an idea, say, of sanctification, we will have to cut out much that God puts in. The irrelevant things in Abraham's life are evidences of that half-unconscious living which proves that his mind was not taken up with himself. The greatest thing in Abraham's life is God, not 'Abraham-ism.' The whole trend of his life is to make us admire God, not Abraham.

The outstanding characteristic in the life of a saint is its irrelevance, an irrelevance which is amazingly relevant to the purpose of God. If you become a devotee to a principle, you become a religious lunatic; you are no longer loyal to the life of Jesus, but loyal only to the logic of your convictions about Him. A fanatic dismisses all irrelevancy in life. We say that a lunatic is a man who has lost his reason; a lunatic is a man who has lost everything but his reason. A madman's explanation of things is always complete. The main thing is life, not logic. It is the irrelevant running all through life that makes it what it is worth.

One of the dangers of the so-called Higher Christian Life movements is the idea that God wants to produce specimens to put in His museum. You can often find better specimens in the world than in the Church. Think of the men and women you know who have not been through the crisis you have been through, and your human reason tells you they are infinitely better than you are, they are more unselfish, never irritable or upset, and yet they would not dream of saying what you have to say, that you are loyal to Jesus Christ. The irrelevancy of your life and the relevancy of theirs will produce perplexity in your mind until

147

you remember that you are not called to produce one of God's specimens; you are called to live in perfect relationship to God so that the net result of your life is not admiration for you, but a longing after God. Christian perfection is not, and never can be, human perfection. Christian perfection is the perfection of a relationship to God which shows itself in the total irrelevancy of human life.

If you get off on the line of personal holiness or Divine healing or the Second Coming of Our Lord, and make any of these your end, you are disloyal to Jesus Christ. Supposing the Lord has healed your body and you make Divine healing your end, the dead set of your life is no longer for God but for what you are pleased to call the manifestation of God in your life. Bother your life! 'It can never be God's will that I should be sick.' If it was God's will to bruise His own Son, why should it not be His will to bruise you? The thing that tells is not relevant consistency to an idea of what a saint's life is, but abandonment abjectly to Jesus Christ whether you are well or ill.

Much of our life is irrelevant to any and every mind saving God's mind. When you obey the call of God the first thing that strikes you is the irrelevancy of the things you have to do, and you are sure to be brought up full butt against the perfect human specimens. The net result of such lives does not leave you with the 'flavour' of God at all, it leaves you with the idea that God is totally unnecessary—by human effort and human devotion we can reach the standard God wants. Well, in a fallen world it cannot be done. Paul refers to this in 2 Cor. iv. 3—4—'the god of this world hath blinded the minds of the unbelieving . . .,' i.e., they have the perfection of the human, but never once have they seen the perfection of God.

Beware of taking your conception of a saint from deductions from certain Scriptures, and always clarify

148

your views by meditation on John xvii. God wants to do with the saints what His Son prayed He would do—make them one with Himself (v. 21).

(II) THE REIGN OF THE IRREVOCABLE. v. 5—7

Ishmael is the son born of the wrong way of doing God's will. If we try to do God's will through our own effort, we produce Ishmael. Much of our modern Christian enterprise is 'Ishmael', i.e., it is born not of God, but of an inordinate desire to do God's will in our own way—the one thing Our Lord never did.

Ishmael, as we have seen, had to be dismissed and disciplined until he was willing to become subservient and be utilized for God's purposes; and the natural has to be put completely under, dismissed and denied, until it is willing to be subjected to God, not to our ideas of relevancy. We put sin in the wrong place. Remember, we cannot touch sin. The Atonement of the Lord alone touches sin. We must not tamper with it for one second. We can do nothing with sin; we must leave God's Redemption to deal with it. Our part has to do with 'Ishmael', i.e., the natural. The natural has to be denied, not because it is bad and wrong, but because it has nothing to do with our life of faith in God until it is turned into the spiritual by obedience. It is the attitude of the maimed life, which so few of us understand.

(III) THE REALM OF THE IRREPROACHABLE. v. 8

The Hebrews regarded life as complete when it was full of days and riches and honour. Age was looked upon as a sign of favour. Whenever a nation becomes unspiritual, it reverses this order, the demand is not for old age but for youth. This reversal in the modern life of to-day is indicative of apostasy, not of advance.

Abraham's life wore to a tranquil sunset. He is described as 'full of years,' i.e., satisfied with life. He had seen, felt, believed, loved, suffered enough, earth had no more to offer him. Through God's goodness he found goodness in everything. Bitterness and cynicism are born of broken gods; bitterness is an indication that somewhere in my life I have belittled the true God and made a god of human perfection.

(IV) THE REUNION OF THE IRRECONCILABLE. v. 9—10
Ishmael and Isaac are re-united at the grave of their father. Ishmael—strong, rugged, human perfection; Isaac—meditative, incomplete visionary, but on the trail of God. These two unite at the burial of Abraham, the Friend of God, whom God will not forsake. 'Gathered to his people' means gathered to the unseen world. This is immortality in direct statement in the Old Testament.

BOOKS BY OSWALD CHAMBERS

	net s. d.	post free s. d.
My Utmost for His Highest	9 6	10 0
Not Knowing Whither (*The Life of Abraham*)	8 6	8 10
The Place of Help (*Devotional Readings*)		
Conformed to His Image		
God's Workmanship	7 6	7 10
The Psychology of Redemption	*each*	
So Send I You (*Missionary Studies*)		
Biblical Psychology		
Outline Studies on "Biblical Psychology"	9	11
Studies in the Sermon on the Mount	6 0	6 4
Baffled to Fight Better (*Book of Job*)	*each*	
He Shall Glorify Me	5 6	5 10
Shade of His Hand (*Book of Ecclesiastes*)	5 0	5 4
Disciples Indeed	*each*	
If Thou wilt be Perfect		
Biblical Ethics	4 6	4 10
If Ye shall Ask	*each*	
The Moral Foundations of Life	4 0	4 4
The Philosophy of Sin	*each*	
The Shadow of an Agony	3 6	3 10
Approved unto God	*each*	
Workmen of God (*The Cure of Souls*)		
Bringing Sons unto Glory	3 0	3 3
(*Studies in the Life of Our Lord*)	*each*	
Facing Reality		
A Little Book of Prayers	2 6	2 9
As He Walked (*Christian Experience*)		
Grow up into Him (*Christian Habits*)		
Our Brilliant Heritage (*Sanctification*)		
Thy Great Redemption	1 6	1 8
The Highest Good	*each*	
The Pilgrim's Song Book		
Talks on the Soul of a Christian		
Called of God		
The Ministry of the Unnoticed	1 3	1 5
The Fighting Chance	*each*	
The Making of a Christian	1 0	1 2
The Patience of the Saints	*each*	
The Discipline Series :		
(1) Divine Guidance, *64 pp.*	1 6	1 8
(2) Suffering, *48 pp.*	1 3	1 5
(3) Loneliness, *72 pp.*	1 9	1 11
(4) Prayer, *64 pp.*	1 6	1 8
(5) Patience, *32 pp.*	9	11
(6) Peril, *64 pp.*	1 6	1 8
The Love of God	9	11
The Message of Invincible Consolation		
Now is it Possible—	*each*	
The Graciousness of Uncertainty		
The Sacrament of Saints	6	8
Oswald Chambers : His Life and Work	10 6	11 0
Seed Thoughts Calendar (*Perpetual*), 7th Series	2 6	2 8